The Wit of

Winston Churchill

GEOFFREY WILLANS

AND

CHARLES ROETTER

MAX PARRISH · LONDON

First published 1954
Reprinted 1955

MAX PARRISH AND CO LTD
55 QUEEN ANNE STREET
LONDON W I

Made and printed in Great Britain by
WILLIAM CLOWES AND SONS LTD
LONDON AND BECCLES

CONTENTS

ILLUSTRATIONS

ACKNOWLEDGEMENTS

The authors wish to express their thanks to the artists who have permitted reproduction of their cartoons in this book, and also to the

News Chronicle
(frontispiece and pp. 31, 43, 53, 58, 91, 105),

the proprietors of *Punch*
(pp. 17, 35, 45, 47, 80, 101),

the *Daily Express* (pp. 15, 94),

the *Daily Mirror* (pp. 49, 65),

the *Manchester Guardian* (pp. 41, 76),

and the

Sunday Times (endpaper).

Sir Winston Churchill first entered Parliament fifty-four years ago. For some of that time he has been – to quote him after his defeat in the 1922 election at Dundee – 'without an office, without a seat, without a party, and without an appendix'. But, in Parliament and out, he has rightly had a reputation for wit.

It is not easy to savour the full flavour of his wit from cold print. The bouquet, for perfection, should be taken in the House itself together with the atmosphere of the occasion and the added effect of gesture, grimace and intonation, for that is the proper arena for the fighter who has noted in himself 'a tendency, against which I should guard, to swim against the stream'.

As a fighter he has used the broadsword, with a gift for repartee as its sharp edge. This has changed very little over the years. His reference to the House of Lords in 1907 as 'this Second Chamber as it is – one-sided, hereditary, irresponsible, absentee' is fashioned with the same workmanship as his devastating dismissal of the Chamberlain Government of nearly thirty years later: 'They are decided only to be undecided, resolved to be irresolute, adamant for drift, all-powerful for impotence.'

This book makes no attempt, however, to give a comprehensive survey of Churchillian wit over the years. Some of the best things of the past have been included, but the main emphasis has been upon the years since he became Prime

Minister again in 1951 – for, in the maturity and sparkle of his mind, these have been the vintage years.

Consider the situation. Prime Minister in his late seventies, re-elected after the acrimonious period of Mr Attlee's Socialist Government, he returned to the Treasury Bench in a position he had not occupied before – a Party Prime Minister, not Prime Minister of a wartime Coalition. In that position he had to expect heavy blows to be aimed at him from the other side of the House. They were, obviously, on topics of the hour – the Korean War, the reversal of political power, the North Atlantic Treaty Organization and the European Defence Community. That he has been able to parry them so successfully is due to several factors – his vast experience of House of Commons tactics, his phenomenal memory (he is once said to have memorized Bartlett's *Familiar Quotations*) and a native gift for repartee.

'Winston's Wit Rocks the House', report headlines in the newspapers. In reading its reproduction, without the frequent cheers, boos and catcalls of Question Time or debate, it is well to realize some limitations. The laughter follows the explosion of the occasion: a reader is more in the position of one who surveys the damage afterwards.

It should not be forgotten, also, that the House of Commons imposes a special form to a battle of a very specialized kind, with rules which are honoured. In reading Sir Winston Churchill's words, therefore, it should be realized that he is speaking a House of Commons language in which he is not by any means the only one to employ *tu quoque* and other thrusts which may appear to belong to the classroom.

Nevertheless, which of the other Members can match him in choice of word and phrase, in irony, in impromptu ability to demolish? In this respect Sir Winston Churchill is the incomparable master, for his shafts have that enviable quality of being always exactly *right*. It is this essential rightness which quotations exemplify.

They give, at any rate, some idea of a master in his finest period. Perhaps it may seem unfair that a man of eighty should sustain attacks which come so thick and fast? To which there are two answers. First, that of a House of Commons expert: 'He can look after himself.' Second, that he still loves every moment of it.

... As if he is enjoying himself hugely!

Question Time

MRS MANN [Labour]: *Is the Prime Minister aware that
. . . the Mint has decided to issue the coins with 'Elizabeth II'
and Scots who object to this title are placed in an awful dilemma?*
THE PRIME MINISTER: *I hope that theoretical refine-
ments will not prevent the normal conduct of business.*
                    [*Hansard, 15 April 1953, col. 200*]

Almost fifty years ago, before the First World War, F. E.
Smith, who later became the first Earl of Birkenhead, once
expressed the view that Sir Winston spent the best years of
his life preparing impromptu remarks. The House of Commons today cares little whether Sir Winston's ripostes are
rehearsed or spontaneous; it is far too intrigued by the unique
spectacle of a Prime Minister employing wit as an adjunct to
statesmanship.

For it is a unique and fairly modern spectacle. Pitt and Gladstone, Asquith and Baldwin, Ramsay MacDonald and Neville Chamberlain – whatever their virtues – brought little laughter to the proceedings at Westminster, and would probably have regarded too sparkling a display of humour as slightly unseemly in a Prime Minister standing at the Despatch Box in the House of Commons.

Not so Sir Winston.

When he announced in 1943 that church bells would no longer be reserved for use as a warning in case of invasion, he was asked what alternative arrangements had been made.

'Replacement does not arise,' came the reply. 'I cannot help thinking that anything like a serious invasion would be bound to leak out.'

During the war such rejoinders were few and far between. Most of Sir Winston's energies were absorbed in the direction of the war, and he was frequently unable to attend the House at Question Time – that hour immediately after the Speaker's prayers at 2.30 when any Member may ventilate a matter of public interest by addressing a Question to a Minister.

It was very different, however, when Sir Winston became Prime Minister for the second time in 1951. Few Prime Ministers in the last thirty years have been as willing to submit themselves to cross-examination on so wide a variety of subjects, and his performance at Question Time has become the star turn of the House.

Even his entry on these occasions is dramatic. Not for him the quick bow to Mr Speaker and the unobtrusive sliding on to the Treasury Bench of the ordinary Minister. His is almost a stately procession.

He usually arrives just after 3 p.m. For by tradition the first Question down to the Prime Minister is never higher in

the list than No. 45, to allow the First Minister of the Crown
to enjoy his lunch at leisure, and by then Question Time has
been in full swing for more than half an hour.

Suddenly there is a bustle of activity behind the Speaker's
Chair. The tall, elegant figure of Mr Patrick Buchan-Hep-
burn, the Government Chief Whip, steps gravely along the
Treasury Bench whispering a hurried warning to the Ministers present. They throw a quick glance in the direction of
the doorway behind Mr Speaker and move over to make
room just by the Despatch Box. Captain Christopher
Soames, Sir Winston's son-in-law and his Parliamentary
Private Secretary, enters, bows to the Chair and takes his seat
immediately behind the space reserved for the Prime Minister. In these few seconds back-benchers and Ministers alike
plainly have some difficulty in concentrating on the subject
under discussion.

And then, almost unexpectedly in spite of all the prepara-
tions, there is Sir Winston himself. He moves slowly, de-
liberately, as if in some ceremony, his shoulders hunched and
his massive head thrust forward. A quick look around the
House, at the Front Bench opposite, at the Opposition bench
just 'below the Gangway' – the base of such irrepressible
Socialist M.P.s as Mr Silverman, Mr Lewis and Mr Bing,
who are only slightly less critical of their own leaders than
of the Tories – at the Conservative benches behind him, at
the Public Gallery, and he slumps down in his seat, fumbling
with his hearing aid.

When Sir Winston first had to resort to hearing aids a few
years ago, he was extremely reluctant to be seen using them
in public. Since then, however, he has come to employ them
as a weapon in debate, like his glasses. When a Member of
the House some time ago tried to provoke him into dropping
a hint about his retirement, he ostentatiously turned to Cap-

tain Soames and asked him to bring him his hearing aid. 'I don't want to miss any of this,' he told the M.P. when it arrived. 'Would you mind repeating what you've just said ?'

At the end of this little scene the House was no wiser about Sir Winston's plans than it had been before.

In theory there is nothing to stop an M.P. from putting down as many Questions as he likes to the Prime Minister, but there is also nothing to compel the Prime Minister to answer even a single one. Yet the House would soon lose confidence in the Head of a Government who persistently refused to face its inquiries. And that is a risk no Government with as slender a majority as Sir Winston's can afford to take.

Not that M.P.s always expect a factual answer to their Questions. They know, as well as the responsible Ministers, that international or defence matters are frequently far too delicate to be discussed in detail across the floor of the House. But they want to see how a Minister handles himself in an awkward situation. Their object is often not so much to elicit information as to advertise themselves and their views or to embarrass and provoke. Rightly or wrongly it is felt that a man who survives the rough and tumble of Question Time, when he may have to face a battery of impromptu queries from all parts of the House without the aid of his advisers and experts, is more likely to be capable of dealing with the Russians or the complexities of Britain's economic or defence problems than one who fails to pass this trying parliamentary test.

Sir Winston's greatest contribution to this sport has been his refusal to seek refuge behind the time-honoured, platitudinous phrases which Ministers are apt to use on these awkward occasions. His shield and his lance in these exchanges has been his wit. It usually enables him to parry the deadliest of thrusts, and in attack he is frequently devastating. Indeed, when he effects a 'kill', his Government's stock, by some curious alchemy of politics, rises noticeably throughout the country.

No one of course enjoys a public drubbing, but it is not unlikely that many an M.P. in years to come will recall the trouncing Sir Winston once gave him as though it were an accolade.

There must be few M.P.s who have not felt the sting of his repartee at some time or other. He can occasionally be merciless, yet most Members end up by laughing with him. And his approach to the variegated assortment of topics in which the duties of his office or personal inclination cause him to take an interest is nothing if not original.

MR GOWER [Conservative]: *Can the Prime Minister state what course will be followed if a future British monarch should bear the name Llewellyn?*
THE PRIME MINISTER: *I hope I may ask for long notice of that question.*   [Hansard, 15 April 1953, col. 200]

The diehard Tory Sir Waldron Smithers has his own brand of question for the Prime Minister:

SIR WALDRON SMITHERS [Conservative]: *Would not the Prime Minister agree that the only way to improve the standards of living of backward races and to avert economic disaster is to allow all peoples to buy in the cheapest and sell in the dearest markets, because if goods cannot cross frontiers, armies will? Will he set the people free?*
THE PRIME MINISTER: *Those seem to me, on the whole, unobjectionable sentiments.*
[Hansard, 23 June 1953, col. 1689]

Among the suggestions with which the Prime Minister is apt to be flooded during Question Time was one to hold a National Day of Prayer.

MR GOWER [Conservative]: *Will the Prime Minister assure the House that, while we have quite properly attended to the physical needs of defence and of our other problems, we should not forget these spiritual resources which have inspired this country in the past and without which the noblest civilization would decay?*

THE PRIME MINISTER: *I hardly think that that is my exclusive responsibility.* [Hansard, 25 March 1952, col. 204]

The Churchill Government's policy of derationing all foodstuffs as quickly as possible after 1951 was watched with considerable misgivings from the Labour benches, and led to many oblique attacks on the Prime Minister.

MR I. O. THOMAS [Labour]: *Will the Prime Minister indicate if he will take the precaution of consulting the consuming public before he decides to abolish the Food Ministry?*

THE PRIME MINISTER: *On the whole, I have always found myself on the side of the consumer.*

[Hansard, 27 Oct. 1953, col. 2623]

Mr Fenner Brockway, the Member for Eton and Slough, is not only a Socialist, but a veteran champion of many causes which are anathema to most Old Etonians. Time has mellowed him since the days in the First World War when he was sent to prison for his opposition to conscription, but he is still ready to cross swords even with so formidable an adversary as Sir Winston – especially if the topic under discussion is the behaviour of American Service men in Britain.

MR FENNER BROCKWAY [Labour]: *Is he (the Prime Minister) aware that . . . the Iver Heath Conservative Party*

Association held a fête to raise money for party purposes to which it invited Service baseball teams, American Service men's teams, to participate for a 'Winston Churchill' trophy, and that the Secretary of the Conservative Party Association is reported locally to have stated that she told the right hon. Gentleman all about the match and had a personal note from him saying that he was honoured that his name was linked with the trophy?

THE PRIME MINISTER: *I read in the 'Daily Worker' some account of this. I was asked whether I would allow my name to be given to a trophy to be presented to the winner of two American Forces' teams that were to play a baseball match at a Conservative fête. I had not, I agree, fully realized the political implications that might attach to the matter, and in so far as I have erred I express my regret.* [Laughter.]

MR H. HYND [Labour]: *While hon. Gentlemen opposite may try to laugh this one off, may I ask whether the Prime Minister would contemplate the attitude of his hon. Friends if this incident had happened in connection with a Labour Party fête?*

THE PRIME MINISTER: *I hope we should all show an equal spirit of tolerance and good humour.*

MR BROCKWAY [Labour]: *Can the Prime Minister estimate what would be the reaction of Mr Eisenhower in America if British Forces participated in a Democratic Party celebration?*

THE PRIME MINISTER: *I certainly should not attempt to add to the many difficult questions which are pending at the present time by bending my mind to the solution of that question.*   [Hansard, 21 July 1952, col. 32]

Mr (now Sir) Robert Boothby, the Member for Aberdeen East, and the Conservative Party's most articulate protagonist on radio and television, asked the Prime Minister to transfer the authority of dealing with foot-and-mouth disease in Scotland from the Ministry of Agriculture in London to the Scottish Office in Edinburgh and met with a point-blank Churchillian refusal.

MR BOOTHBY: *Is my right hon. Friend aware that there is a torrent of complaints from Scotland at the present time?*
THE PRIME MINISTER: *I am sure my hon. Friend would be fully capable of giving full vent to any such torrent, but the difficulty is that we are not sure that foot-and-mouth disease is as well educated on the subject of borders and questions arising out of them as he is.*
MR BOOTHBY: *I beg to give notice that I shall raise this matter on the Adjournment.*
THE PRIME MINISTER: *I am afraid I cannot undertake to be present when this new red herring is drawn across the Border.* [*Hansard, 6 May 1952, col.* 186]

On the decision to return the Coronation Stone to Westminster Abbey, the Prime Minister scored against Emrys Hughes, who has travelled in Russia, with a reference to the 'Red Dean'.

MR EMRYS HUGHES [Labour]: *Is the Prime Minister aware . . . that the Dean of Westminster is now wondering whether, on the Day of Judgment, he will appear with the Prime Minister on a charge of accepting stolen property?*
THE PRIME MINISTER: *I should have thought that the hon. Member would be more concerned with the future of the Dean of Canterbury.* [*Hansard, 3 March 1952, col.* 28]

When the 'Red Dean' returned from the Soviet Union and Communist China claiming to have 'cast-iron evidence' of American germ warfare in Korea and North China, Sir Winston refused to have him tried for treason and imprisoned, as some Members of the House suggested.

THE PRIME MINISTER: *Free speech carries with it the evil of all foolish, unpleasant and venomous things that are said, but on the whole we would rather lump them than do away with them.* [Hansard, 15 July 1952, col. 1978]

The arrangements for the Coronation came under close scrutiny. When Mr Glanville (Labour) suggested that contingents representing all aspects of industrial life should be included in the Coronation Procession in order to make the Procession fully representative of the industrial as well as the military power of Britain, he did not find Sir Winston particularly sympathetic.

THE PRIME MINISTER: *The arrangements for the Procession are in the hands of the Coronation Committee and I expect that they will recommend that only military formations should be included.*
HON. MEMBERS: *Why?*
THE PRIME MINISTER: *You must think of the spectators.*
[Hansard, 18 Nov. 1952, col. 1585]

An intervention by Sir Waldron Smithers in the course of one of the many serious and sombre discussions on the British atom bomb tests in Australia allowed Sir Winston to strike a lighter note.

SIR WALDRON SMITHERS [Conservative]: *When the day is fixed, will the Prime Minister arrange for a number of fellow travellers, including Members of this House and of the Church, to be on the site? If he likes, I will send him a preliminary list.*

THE PRIME MINISTER: *I am well aware of the widespread interest that is taken in what I may call the utilitarian employment of nuclear energy, but I think it would have to be administered on a bi-partisan basis.*

[*Hansard*, 10 July 1952, *col.* 1517]

An exasperated Labour Member's suggestion that the Prime Minister should remove Sir Waldron Smithers from the House and leave him in Bermuda, enabled Sir Winston to score off both parties to the dispute.

MR SHURMER [Labour]: *Will the right hon. Gentleman consider taking the hon. Member for Orpington (Sir Waldron Smithers) with him, as it would please both sides of the House if he would take him and leave him there?*
SIR WALDRON SMITHERS [Conservative]: *On a point of order. May I tell you, Mr Speaker, that I take no objection to that, but I wish the hon. Member for Sparkbrook (Mr Shurmer) would go away too.*
THE PRIME MINISTER: *I will try to answer that question. I earnestly hope that it will be arranged through the usual channels so that equal numbers on both sides of the House have this unfortunate experience offered to them.*

[*Hansard*, 23 June 1953, *col.* 1689]

M.P.s ask roughly 10,000 Questions a year, but there would be little hope of having anything like that number answered, if the Mother of Parliaments had not adopted a neat, time-saving device. The first Question on any topic is never read out. It is printed on the pale-green Order Paper of the House, and when its turn comes, the Speaker calls on the Member who put it down, the Member announces briefly, 'No. 29', or 'No. 43', and the Minister to whom the Question is addressed goes straight into his reply. Unlike

supplementary questions and Ministerial answers, the original
question is always reported in indirect speech.

MR HECTOR HUGHES [Labour] *asked the Prime Minister
if he will reconsider his refusal to separate the Ministry of
Agriculture from the Ministry of Fisheries, in view of the
national importance of the fishing industry; and if he will
now take steps to set up a separate Ministry to solve its
problems and attend to its development.*

THE PRIME MINISTER: *It would not, I feel, be a good arrangement to have a separate Department for every industry of
national importance. These two industries have been long
associated departmentally and, after all, there are many
ancient links between fish and chips.*

[*Hansard, 17 June 1954, col. 2289*]

Members periodically press the Prime Minister for information about the chances of holding a meeting between the
Heads of the British, American and Russian Governments.
On one occasion a Question on this topic coincided with the
sensational arrest in Moscow of a number of Russian doctors
for the alleged poisoning of certain leading Soviet personalities.

MR EMRYS HUGHES [Labour]: *Has the Prime Minister
forgotten that in at least half a dozen important speeches on
the eve of the last Election he pressed for a meeting with Mr
Stalin? Is he aware that earlier in this year Mr Stalin declared himself favourably towards a meeting? Why does the
Prime Minister now run away? Why does he not unite with
Mr Stalin, and invite President Eisenhower?*

THE PRIME MINISTER: *I think we must try to understand
the general position as it moves. We in this country would feel*

very severe domestic preoccupations, making it difficult to have conversations with heads of Governments, if, for instance, so many of our best doctors were being charged with poisoning so many of our best politicians.

[*Hansard, 9 Feb. 1953, col. 28*]

Charges of bad faith in bringing about a Big Three Meeting usually produce a Churchillian thunderbolt.

MR DODDS [Labour]: *Does the right hon. Gentleman deny that he himself some years ago made a statement as to what he would do if he got the power? He has had it for 18 months and he has done nothing in that respect.*

THE PRIME MINISTER: *I did not get the power to regulate the way in which the affairs of the world would go. I only got the power to preside over a party which has been able to beat the Opposition in Divisions for 18 months.*

[*Hansard, 22 April 1953, col. 1171*]

On another occasion a similar Question was put down while the Western Powers and the Soviet bloc were negotiating at Geneva.

MR DODDS [Labour] *asked the Prime Minister if, in view of the present international situation, he will reconsider taking the initiative in an effort to arrange a meeting at top level, representing the United States of America, the Union of Soviet Socialist Republics and this country, in an attempt to lessen the tension.*

THE PRIME MINISTER: *Perhaps on this somewhat delicate topic I may be permitted by the House to take refuge in metaphor. Many anxieties have been expressed recently at the severe character of the course of the Grand National steeple-*

chase, but I am sure that it could not be improved by asking
the horses to try to jump two fences at the same time.
                    [*Hansard, 17 June 1954, col. 2291*]

One of the Labour Opposition's favourite pastimes is to
imply that the Conservatives have honoured none of the
pledges on which they were elected in 1951. Where, they
used to ask, is the red meat the Tories promised? What
about Commonwealth and Empire development which
figured so prominently in the Conservative election mani-
festo? Sir Winston usually disposes of these gambits with
little difficulty.

MR GORDON WALKER [Labour]: *Does the right hon.*
Gentleman's answer mean that the part of 'Britain Strong
and Free' which set out Conservative Party policy on the
Commonwealth in the Election has now been abandoned?
THE PRIME MINISTER: *Nothing that we set out in our*
statement of policy before the Election has now been aban-
doned, and we all look forward to the moment when we shall
be able to ram red meat down the throats of hon. Members
opposite.   [*Hansard, 8 July 1952, col. 1095*]

Each day's sitting of the House begins with the formal
procession of Mr Speaker. As he leaves his rooms to make
his way through the Central Hall and the Members' Lobby
to the Chamber, preceded by a white-gloved Messenger, and
the Serjeant at Arms carrying the Mace, the symbol of the
authority of the House, and followed by his Train-bearer, his
Chaplain and his Secretary, the corridors and lobbies resound
with the cry: 'Speaker-r-r! Speaker-r-r!' Everyone rises to
his feet, policemen stand at attention, and visitors doff their
hats and bow respectfully, as the representative and spokes-

man of the Commons slowly passes by in his full-bottomed wig and black silk gown.

Ancient custom and tradition are in evidence even during prayers, to which the public is never admitted. For to this day Members turn their back on the Speaker and his Chaplain, kneeling not on the floor but on the benches – a relic of the times when men wore swords.

Another reminder of those days are the two red lines immediately in front of the Government and Opposition front benches. They are sufficiently far apart to make it impossible for two men with drawn swords to reach each other, and even today no Member, addressing the House, may set foot beyond them – save at the cost of uproar.

Those red lines show the real character of the House. It is an arena of battle. Strength today lies only in mental agility. It is brought to fighting trim by experience, memory, understanding, and even sensitiveness. Once the training is there, the contestants must proceed, as do other fighters, by employing their instinct in the ring.

Soon after taking office again in 1951, Sir Winston reduced his own and other Ministerial salaries to set the nation an example of voluntary economy. Lt.-Col. Lipton (Labour) described his action as 'a hollow gesture'.

THE PRIME MINISTER: *I am looking forward to seeing the hon. and gallant Gentleman make a gesture of which it can be said that it is at any rate not less hollow.*

MR W. WYATT [Labour]: *Is it not a fact that when Income Tax has been deducted the saving is relatively negligible, and would it not be more appropriate if at his time of life the Prime Minister abandoned these cheap demagogic gestures?*

THE PRIME MINISTER: *I think the hon. Gentleman is a*

ARENA OF BATTLE

Vicky's cartoon 'I spy strangers', 27 July 1950

judge of cheap demagogic gestures, but they do not often come off when he makes them.

MR SHINWELL [Labour]: *In view of the castigations of the right hon. Gentleman on the Members of the former Government does he not realize that, even at the reduced salary, the Members of his Government are not worth it?*

THE PRIME MINISTER: *The right hon. Gentleman is no doubt trying to live up to the cheap demagogic gestures mentioned by his hon. Friend. [Hansard, 29 July 1952, col. 1264]*

Mr Harold Davies, the Labour Member for Leek, Staffordshire, found that it served little purpose getting exasperated if Sir Winston felt he ought to withhold information on the Korean war for military or diplomatic reasons.

MR HAROLD DAVIES [Labour]: *Does the right hon. Gentleman realize that the House is getting less information on the Korean situation than his equally great predecessor Mr Gladstone was giving the House in the time of the Crimean War?*

THE PRIME MINISTER: *I am afraid I have not at my fingers' ends the exact part which Mr Gladstone took in the Crimean War; it was even before my time.*

[*Hansard, 28 May 1952, col. 1372*]

The art of stating the unpleasant truth without provoking a diplomatic incident was demonstrated by the Prime Minister when he was asked where all the jet 'planes and self-propelling guns of the North Koreans came from.

SIR WALDRON SMITHERS [Conservative]: *Moscow.*

THE PRIME MINISTER: *Although there are movements ever being made in aerial locomotion, it would be premature to suppose that they came from the moon.*

[*Hansard, 28 May 1952, col. 1373*]

Mr Lewis (Labour), who usually sits on the Opposition front bench 'just below the gangway' and is frequently as critical of the leaders of his own Party as of the Government, suggested that the nation was far from satisfied with the conduct of affairs in Korea.

MR LEWIS [Labour]: *Is the Prime Minister aware of the deep concern felt by the people of this country at the whole question of the Korean conflict . . . ?*

THE PRIME MINISTER: *I am fully aware of the deep concern felt by the hon. Member in many matters above his comprehension.*

[*Hansard, 18 Nov. 1952, col. 1585*]

Various Opposition M.P.s were trying to persuade Sir Winston to abandon the idea of reintroducing University

seats, which had been abolished by the previous Labour
Government, and Mr Lewis (Labour) was looking for a
chance to get his own back after the blow which Sir Winston
had administered on the previous day.

MR M. STEWART [Labour]: *Will the Prime Minister
remember the Greek proverb, 'Much learning does not teach
sense'?*
MR LEWIS [Labour]: *May I ask the Prime Minister
whether that is above his comprehension?*
THE PRIME MINISTER: *I am sorry to see that I hit so
deeply home.*   [*Hansard, 19 Nov. 1952, col. 18*]

Mr Douglas Jay, one of the band of Socialist economists
with academic backgrounds who had been responsible for
many of the Labour Government's blueprints for Britain's
economic future, raised the question of what steps the
Government was taking to guard against unemployment.
Sir Winston's answer was evasive.

MR JAY [Labour]: *Would we be right in inferring from
the Prime Minister's answer that he himself has given no
thought to this question?*
THE PRIME MINISTER: *That would be a rather hazardous
assumption on the part of the right hon. Gentleman, who has
not, so far as I am aware, at any time in his Parliamentary
career distinguished himself for foresight.*
                     [*Hansard, 23 July 1952, col. 533*]

Mr Nally (Labour), who has never been very popular
with the Prime Minister, asked Sir Winston to define Lord
Woolton's Ministerial duties. The Prime Minister showed
himself singularly uncommunicative.

C

MR NALLY: *Will the Prime Minister not tell us – or does he himself not know?*

MR SHINWELL [Labour]: *Will the Prime Minister tell us why he has suddenly become so shy? Usually he is very anxious to add a great deal on supplementary questions. Could he not expand a little on this occasion? What is the matter with him?*

THE PRIME MINISTER: *I have to measure the length of the response to any supplementary question by the worth, meaning and significance of that supplementary question.*

[*Hansard*, 18 *June* 1952, *col.* 1199]

Lt.-Col. Lipton raised the Question of which Governments had been invited to send observers to the British atom bomb tests in Australia.

THE PRIME MINISTER: *None, sir.*

LT.-COL. LIPTON [Labour]: *Is it not desirable at a time when the economic and other relationships between the Commonwealth countries are more disrupted than ever they have been, that in this respect at any rate, they should be brought into consideration which would enable Commonwealth observers to be present, if not Australian observers? May I ask the Prime Minister if he will condescend to answer that question, because it seems that Commonwealth relations are involved to some extent? If he is not interested in the matter, then, of course, he need not answer the question.*

THE PRIME MINISTER: *It was after full consideration of all those points that I gave my somewhat comprehensive or rather exclusively comprehensive answer 'None, sir'.*

[*Hansard*, 21 *May* 1952, *col.* 472]

Panorama

Only once during his Parliamentary career is it recorded that Winston Churchill was forced to borrow a witty phrase from another man. In mitigation, this was as he was waiting in the sick, nervous tension that preceded his maiden speech. It was the young Churchill's third day in Parliament and he had planned to speak of the Boer War. Lloyd George, an equally young man, rose excitedly to his feet before Churchill was due to speak and embarked upon an animated and violent impromptu speech. Winston Churchill confesses that he was at a loss to know what reference to make when Lloyd George should sit down. He was groping in vain for something to say, when a Conservative member on his left, Mr Thomas Gibson Bowles, leaned across:

'You might say,' he suggested, '"Instead of making his violent speech without moving his moderate amendment, he had better have moved his moderate amendment without making his violent speech."'

Churchill realized this was good enough and jumped to his feet. To his surprise Lloyd George gracefully gave way and the Churchill maiden speech went off to the general approval of a critical House. Churchill had the credit for the remark. Many years later, however, he was at pains to acknowledge the source of wit borrowed from the same man. This was during his Budget Speech of 1929, when he opposed Lloyd George's proposals to overcome unemployment by embarking on large-scale public works.

'The detailed method of spending the money has not yet been fully thought out, but we are assured on the highest authority that if only enough resource and energy is used there will be no difficulty in getting rid of the stuff. This is the policy which used to be stigmatized by the late Mr Thomas Gibson Bowles as the policy of buying a biscuit early in the morning and walking about all day looking for a dog to give it to.'

These two instances apart, Winston Churchill has needed no assistance in minting his own phrases. Throughout the years they have clinked out steadily, for his humour is native and cannot be restrained for long without bubbling out.

He has used it in various ways – against himself, to bring in homely touches, to prick an opponent's egotism and sometimes with a touch of slapstick. He has used it at times, too, in the most crushing and devastating way. Perhaps the best example of this is his well-known and tremendous indictment of the ineffectual Prime Minister Ramsay Macdonald. In a speech in the House in January 1933, he said:

'I remember, when I was a child, being taken to the celebrated Barnum's Circus, which contained an exhibition of freaks and monstrosities, but the exhibit on the programme which I most desired to see was the one described as "The Boneless Wonder". My parents judged that that spectacle would be too revolting and demoralizing for my youthful eyes, and I have waited fifty years to see the Boneless Wonder sitting on the Treasury Bench.'

This was savage indictment of the 'greatest living master of falling without hurting himself'. When the target is smaller the humour is less ferocious. In 1949 the earnest Mr Harold Davies, the Member for Leek, had cause to interrupt Churchill in debate, when he, as Leader of the Opposition, was defending his plea made at Strasbourg, for the inclusion of Germany in the European family.

MR WINSTON CHURCHILL: . . . *and on 9th November, the week before last, it was announced that this committee were also unanimously in favour of the admission of Germany provided that the new German Government indicated its wish and ability to comply with the democratic conditions of membership.*

MR HAROLD DAVIES [Labour]: *May I interrupt the right hon. Gentleman? This is of vital importance. I put this question in no partisan spirit whatever. [Laughter.] Hon. Members opposite need not smile – this is vital to the destiny and peace of the world. Is the right hon. Gentleman prepared to take the risk of completely rearming Germany at this juncture, because that is what his proposal ultimately means.*

HON. MEMBERS: *Nonsense.*

MR CHURCHILL: *I must leave the House to judge of the total lack of connection between what the hon. Member has said and any language being used by me, or anything in the immediate circumstances before us in Europe.*

[*Hansard*, 17 *Nov.* 1949, *col.* 2230]

Such total demolition has been repeated on other occasions. Once during a speech a Member became so incensed with what Churchill was saying that he jumped to his feet and tried to protest. So deep, however, were his feelings that the only sound to emerge was a gurgle. 'My right honourable Friend', observed Mr Churchill, looking round, 'should not develop more indignation than he can contain.'

As an interrupter himself, he once scored a bullseye against the late Sir William Joynson-Hicks. Hicks was in the middle of a speech when he saw Churchill lounging back on the Opposition Front Bench, shaking his head vigorously. 'I see my right honourable Friend shaking his head,' observed Joynson-Hicks, irritably. 'I wish to remind him that I am only expressing my own opinion.'

'And I', replied Churchill, 'wish to remind the speaker that I am only shaking my own head.'

Part of the politician's art which Winston Churchill mastered very early was that of using 'Parliamentary language'. This, briefly, is the House of Commons' own elaborate code of courtesy. Thus, an opponent is always referred to as 'the honourable Gentleman', a member of the same party as 'honourable Friend'. If he belongs to Her Majesty's Privy Council (as do all Ministers and ex-Ministers) the reference is 'right honourable', whilst direct terms of abuse such as 'cad', 'fool' or 'liar' are completely out of order. Such necessary restraints, however, have never cramped Sir Winston Churchill, who regards them as a challenge to his ingenuity. When certain Socialist Members at one period immediately after the war constantly interrupted him with jeers, he made a typical aside in the best House of Commons tradition.

MR WINSTON CHURCHILL: *The crackling of thorns beneath the pot does not disturb me!*

Those who recognized the Biblical reference, which occurs in Ecclesiastes VII, 6, found that the full quotation read:

'For as the crackling of thorns under a pot, so is the laughter of a fool'

Perhaps the most famous illustration of this studied employment of Parliamentary language came in 1906, very early in his career. One of the issues in the General Election of that year had been the alleged importation of 'Chinese slaves' to work in the Rand mines. Churchill said in a speech in the House:

> It cannot, in the opinion of His Majesty's Government, be classified as slavery in the extreme acceptance of the word without some risk of terminological inexactitude.

But if this is a refinement of wit the opposite extreme has often tempted him. Indeed, he has been known to surprise everyone with a sudden and complete abandonment of Parliamentary custom. When David Kirkwood, the fiery Socialist Member from Glasgow, was showing tempestuous signs of disagreement during a speech, Churchill suddenly stopped in the middle and said: 'Now, Davie, behave yourself.' It is reported that Kirkwood made no further interjections.

Once, during a speech to a packed chamber, an obscure Socialist member wanted to get a paper from the desk which stands between Government and Opposition Front benches. Trying to be as inconspicuous as possible he went down on all fours, but Churchill noticed him. His eyes travelled, he stopped his speech and then, leaning over the desk, he demanded: 'Well, where did *you* come from?' No schoolboy held to ridicule before the whole class could have been more discomfited.

Against this, has anyone scored a knockdown blow on Churchill? Plenty have tried, for it is not easy, in his present phase of honour, to think of him as he has been during his past Parliamentary career: distrusted as brilliant but unsound during the nineteen thirties and, at the outset of his career, disliked for being pushing and bumptious. Indeed, it was during this early phase that one of the few scores against Churchill that have stuck was made. Churchill had angered his own party, the Conservatives, by his independent views on free trade. In the Parliamentary session of 1903 his own party demonstrated against him by leaving the House in a body when he rose to speak. They even paused to jeer at him from the doorway. It was left to a Conservative, Claude Lowther, to put this feeling into words. Informing the House that beriberi had broken out in South Africa, Lowther suggested that Churchill had contracted it.

He added: 'I made that remark because I have heard that the most marked characteristic sympton of the disease is a terrific swelling of the head.'

Previously, however, Churchill had done much better than this. Of Joseph Chamberlain he said: 'Mr Chamberlain loves the working man, he loves to see him work.' And when the blimpish Colonel Kenyon-Slaney bluntly called him a 'traitor' there was no mercy in the reply.

'I have noticed', said Churchill, 'that when political controversy becomes excited, persons of choleric dispositions and limited intelligence are apt to become rude. If I was a traitor, at any rate I was fighting the Boers in South Africa when Colonel Kenyon-Slaney was slandering them at home. I had the honour of serving in the field for our country while this gallant fire-eating colonel was content to kill Kruger with his mouth in the comfortable security of England.'

In the mellowness of attainment and success, Sir Winston has even allowed his humour to flash back on himself.

'Much better to leave the past to history'

'For my part,' he declared in 1948, 'I consider that it will be found much better by all parties to leave the past to history, especially as I propose to write that history myself.'

There is still plenty of political fire left. And he can still keep the whole world guessing. But you can at least have a pretty good idea what Churchill will do by looking at the trends of his life.

First of all, he is a fighter. He hates war, but enjoys fighting. 'Never give in,' he told the boys of Harrow, his old school, 'never, never, never.' When he first joined the army as a subaltern in 1895 he found that there was plenty of time on his hands – the military year was divided into seven months of training and five months' leave. There was no war or prospect of one to make such an arrangement scandalous – indeed, there is quite a bit to be said for concentrating service inactivity into one spell to allow something more useful to be done. In Churchill's case he made a simple decision. If there was not a war, he would go and look for one. He went off first as a special correspondent to a tinpot revolution in Cuba, and later, after a year or two with the Fourth Hussars in India, he pulled strings to get himself to the Pathan revolution on the northern frontier of India. The result of this was a book, *The Story of the Malakand Field Force,* published in 1898, so broad in scope and liberal with criticism that it was suggested its title should be changed to *A Subaltern's Hints to Generals.*

It took a further visit to the Sudanese war and his famous escapades against the Boers to emphasize to his contemporaries what is tolerably well known to ourselves – that his second characteristic is that he can take nothing for granted. He never looks without asking what better can be done. This was, in fact, what he was doing in his famous memoranda during the war – they might almost pass as 'A Prime Minister's Demands on Generals'.

It is in his nature to make the most of his tremendous abilities, but equally he can score points with defects. At Harrow he was a poor scholar of Latin, in India he was unable to learn, and the only things about his French are its wide vocabulary and execrable accent. Yet this is typically Churchillian.

'*Prenez garde!* I am going to speak in French,' he declared in his speech at the liberation of Paris ' – a formidable undertaking and one which will put great demands upon your friendship for Great Britain.' At another period during the war he is said to have described a detachment of the Women's Voluntary Service as '*des femmes gratuites*' which caused

Cabinet meeting, 1952

the Frenchman to whom he said it to recount the matter at
his embassy, adding, '*Mon Dieu, quelle situation!*' As an
American commented: 'He had apparently never seen before what he took to be female camp followers dressed in
pretty uniforms and drilling in the streets.'

Some of all this makes up the alchemy of this last surviv-
ing aristocrat of the ruling classes. In recent Parliaments he
has had this advantage of dealing with adversaries from a
height, yet no man has been so unyielding in his determina-
tion that the democratic nature of the Commons should be
preserved.

'We shape our dwellings and afterwards our dwellings
shape us,' he said, during a speech on the rebuilding of the
bomb-damaged House.

The Chamber, destroyed by fire and high-explosive bombs, has now arisen on the older model. It looks and smells new, in strong contrast to the Lords, which looks and smells old. Various parts of the appurtenances of the new Commons Chamber have come from the Commonwealth and Empire: but the important fact is that, owing to Winston Churchill's influence, it is still too small to contain in its seats all the Members of Parliament. Churchill and many others agree that this has an important atmospheric bearing: on a great occasion, with members crowded in (even sitting on each other's knees), the proper tension is generated; on the more frequent lesser occasions the desolation of sparse attendance is less evident. As a result, the new and old Chambers have a curious compound in common – they are still the most frightening arenas in the world for a maiden speaker, still critical of those who fail and appreciative of those who are reasonable and just according to their lights.

The bitterest blow which ever came to him in his life, his rejection by the electorate in the victory election of 1945, he has described vividly and painfully. Yet even this could serve as a source for a witty phrase, albeit a somewhat wan one. Speaking at the Lord Mayor's Banquet at the Guildhall just after his electoral victory of 1951, he said:

'This is the first occasion when I have addressed this assembly here as a Prime Minister. The explanation is convincing. When I should have come here as Prime Minister the Guildhall was blown up and before it was repaired I was blown out.'

There can never be a good statue of Sir Winston Churchill. A statue means repose, one set of countenance, one frame of mind: it cannot reproduce the orator, the actor, the sentimentalist, the soldier, the tyrant and all the other pieces

His twinkling eyes seemed to say,
'I do look a bit of a sight, I expect'

45

which make up the fabric of this extraordinary man. Above all it will never reflect the puckish element that glints suddenly and irresistibly out of his eye even in the most solemn moment. No one could be more deeply conscious of the honour bestowed upon him when he was installed as a Companion of the Most Noble Order of the Garter at Windsor Castle. Yet as he walked between the crowds in slow procession down the Lower Ward of the Castle clad in voluminous cap of ostrich feather and the magnificent mantle of the Order his set face on occasion suddenly broke, and his twinkling eyes seemed to say, 'I do look a bit of a sight, I expect.'

This is the quality which makes people acclaim him as 'Good old Winnie'. It was what made him delight everyone with references to 'Corporal Schicklgruber' during the war. It made him pronounce Nazis as 'Narzis' and gave birth to his immortal exclamation, 'Some chicken – some neck!' It is, in short, his Englishness.

'We are like a lot of sheep, aren't we?' Mr Maurice Webb, the Socialist, observed to him once.

'Yes, bloody black sheep,' grunted Winston Churchill.

Right Honourable Opponents

THE PRIME MINISTER: *I can assure the right hon. Gentleman [Mr Herbert Morrison] that the spectacle of a number of middle-aged gentlemen who are my political opponents being in a state of uproar and fury is really quite exhilarating to me.*

[*Hansard, 21 May 1952, col. 531*]

Sir Winston likes Clement Attlee. The two learnt to respect one another's qualities during the war and even the dust raised by the heated political battles at Westminster after the war never obliterated the bond of loyalty that developed between them then. Sir Winston has repeatedly spoken of Mr Attlee's 'concise, massive, statesmanlike contribution' to a better international understanding, and Mr Attlee seems to enjoy the occasions when he can – as he puts it drily – 'once again support' Sir Winston in some cause or other.

Yet the two men have never been intimate – a circumstance due not so much to differences in political outlook as in temperament. Unlike Mr Attlee, Sir Winston revels in turning even the drabbest, most commonplace occurrence into an Occasion.

During Mr Attlee's Premiership it fell to him, as Leader of the Opposition, to inquire each Thursday after Question Time what business the Government intended to put before the House in the coming week. Ordinarily, this inquiry is merely a matter of routine, and now that Mr Attlee is Leader of the Opposition, the question certainly never varies from one Parliamentary session to the next. In Sir Winston's Opposition days, however, the question was never the same in two consecutive weeks.

Sometimes he would put it as if he could barely summon sufficient courage to lay so frivolous a request before a mighty, all-powerful Government; at other times he would fling it across the floor of the House like a challenge, as if he dared the Government to expose its dastardly plans for all to see; and now and again the tone of his question would suggest that it was useless to expect Mr Attlee's Administration to know its own mind even on a routine matter.

During his period in Opposition he frequently conveyed the impression that he considered Mr Attlee and his Cabinet to be personally responsible to him. So much so that on one occasion Mr Herbert Morrison reminded him acidly that 'another right hon. Gentleman now presides over the Cabinet'.

Sir Winston was not in the least taken aback. 'I am quite willing to recognize the fact – such as it is!'

But the former Labour Prime Minister's survival, for almost 20 years, as leader of a Party which periodically indulges in noisy and much publicized fratricidal warfare, leads one to suspect that he can take care of himself in most situations.

Accused, shortly after his Party's sweeping victory in 1945, of allowing Britain to fall behind in the 'revolution' brought about by atomic development, he replied tersely: 'We do not intend to be left behind in any revolution.'

For all his modesty Mr Attlee is not easily flattened. Few people ever get the better of him in the cut and thrust of debate. He rarely

'Always ready to commiserate with Mr Attlee'

intervenes unless he feels he has something to say, and one senses that he expects others to do likewise. Indeed, there is in his crisp, dry, unemotional voice something of the headmaster, sure of himself and his authority. And there is enough of the irrepressible schoolboy in Sir Winston to try his hardest to undermine the 'Head's' authority.

Failing that, he is always ready to commiserate with Mr Attlee on the trials and tribulations which the leadership of the Labour Party appears to entail. In a debate on the general policy of the Churchill Government, Mr Attlee had just delivered a rousing attack on the Prime Minister and his colleagues which had delighted all sections of the Labour Party.

THE PRIME MINISTER: *A great deal of his speech was made up of very effective points and quips which gave a great deal of satisfaction to those behind him. We all understand his position:* 'I am their leader, I must follow them.'

[*Hansard, 6 Nov. 1951, col.* 68]

D

In the debate on the Queen's Speech setting out the Government's policy for the coming Session, Mr Attlee, on behalf of the Opposition, subjected the Speech to a careful scrutiny.

MR ATTLEE [Labour]: *I note the passage on the unity of Europe. I am glad to see that the Government have very largely come to take the same line as that which the Labour Government took. There was a time when it looked as though the Prime Minister was going to be, so to speak, stroke of the European boat, but he is now only offering a few helpful suggestions from the towpath . . .*

THE PRIME MINISTER: *Now we have had a speech, as is customary on these occasions, from the Leader of the Opposition, and I can only hope that the moderation and sobriety of his statement will not expose him to any undue risk among his own friends. I am sure I may offer him my congratulations on his being able to address us from those benches as stroke and not, to quote the term he has just used, from the towpath.*

[*Hansard, 4 Nov. 1952, col. 20*]

Following the announcement by Sir Winston that two Government departments were to be amalgamated, the Opposition pressed him – without success – to tell them how much money would be saved by this move.

MR ATTLEE [Labour]: *Are we to understand from the Prime Minister that these changes are not based on carefully ascertained facts?*

THE PRIME MINISTER: *Considering the awful mess that the right hon. Gentleman and his colleagues made of our affairs during their many years of almost absolute power, I marvel at their effrontery.*

MR ATTLEE: *The right hon. Gentleman has often heard,*
'No case, abuse the other side.'
THE PRIME MINISTER: *With great respect, I would ask*
your permission, Mr Speaker, to correct the misquotation –
'When you have no case, abuse the plaintiff's attorney.'

[Hansard, 26 Feb. 1953, col. 2330]

In one of his speeches Sir Winston had to refer to a col-
league of his, Mr Harold Macmillan. Unable to mention him
by name, under the rules of the House, he tried to remember
the rather cumbersome title of the Ministry which Mr Macmillan headed.

THE PRIME MINISTER: *My right hon. Friend the*
Minister for Housing and Town Planning –
HON. MEMBERS: *No.*
THE PRIME MINISTER: *Give it me again.*
MR ATTLEE: *Minister for Housing and Local Government.*
THE PRIME MINISTER: *I am much obliged to the right hon.*
Gentleman; there is nothing like getting it accurate.

[Hansard, 1 July 1952, col. 282]

During his term as Prime Minister, Mr Attlee had
abolished the University seats, and he was now urging
Sir Winston not to restore them.

MR ATTLEE [Labour]: *Has the Prime Minister not*
always put the point of university seats not from the
national point of view but from the hope that it would give
him a majority?
THE PRIME MINISTER: *I have frequently disagreed very*
much with some of the statements made by university Mem-
bers. Of course it may be that the trend of things is to put the

*most gifted intellectuals in this country more solidly upon the
Conservative side. That, no doubt, is an explanation of the
right hon. Gentleman's change of position.*

[*Hansard*, 20 Oct. 1953, col. 1813]

Mr Herbert Morrison

DEPUTY LEADER OF THE OPPOSITION

In 1949 Mr Morrison had been Deputy Prime Minister,
Leader of the House of Commons and Lord President of the
Council in the post-war Labour Government for more than
four years. Yet when he went to Strasbourg for the opening
of the Council of Europe, the French police, clearing a way
for Sir Winston, moved him along with the rest of the
crowd, and even after a week in Strasbourg there were still
many Frenchmen who, at the mention of Mr Morrison's
name, would inquire politely: '*Qui est M. Morrison?*'

It was an unkind blow, but then Mr Morrison's excursions
into foreign affairs have never been particularly happy. On
the one occasion after the Conservative victory in 1951, on
which he seriously ventured to attack the Government's
foreign policy, he heard Sir Winston dismiss his speech as
a 'weak, vague, wandering harangue which at no point
touched the realities'.

There is no doubt that he feels much happier on his home
ground, particularly the Chamber of the Commons and the
corridors and committee rooms of the Palace of Westminster. During Labour's term of power he persuaded, cajoled,
jollied and bullied the Commons into tackling the heaviest
legislative programme of any Parliament in British history.
Sir Winston, who came to value his organizing ability during the war when he was Home Secretary in charge of Civil

Defence, once described him as a 'master craftsman' – a remark which Herbert Morrison was ready to accept as a compliment until Sir Winston added mischievously: 'Craft is common both to skill and deceit.'

Certainly Sir Winston has never felt it incumbent upon himself to ease Mr Morrison's difficulties. When the lobbies at Westminster were buzzing with rumours of rifts within the Labour Government, he spoke of him as 'a man outpassed at the moment by his competitors, outdated even by his prejudices' and adapted Lord Tennyson's famous lines to describe his dilemma:

'Master craftsman'

> Crippses to right of him,
> Daltons to left of him,
> Bevans behind him
> Volleyed and thundered.

To outsiders, who are inclined to believe that the House of Commons ceased being 'the best Club in Europe' long ago, it may come as a surprise that the two men should still be on speaking terms after such hammer blows. Yet when over-

work caused Mr Morrison to fall seriously ill with thrombo-
sis, Sir Winston sent flowers to his hospital ward to cheer
him up.

Shortly afterwards Sir Winston himself fell ill, and by
pure chance both returned to the House on the same day.
Members irrespective of their party allegiance, gave a cheer,
as first Sir Winston and a few minutes later Mr Morrison
entered the Chamber, and then witnessed the curious spectacle of each glancing shyly and surreptitiously across at the
other, uncertain of the best way of renewing contact after
their illnesses.

Finally, Mr Morrison could stand it no longer. He rushed
across the floor of the House, grabbed Sir Winston's hand
and told his old wartime Chief how glad he was to see him
back. Sir Winston flushed with pleasure.

There was a more formal exchange of pleasantries a few
moments later. Sir Winston expressed the hope that Mr
Morrison's labours would not prove too much for him. 'I
speak, of course, in a purely physical and not a political
sense.'

And Mr Morrison, complimenting Sir Winston on his remarkable recovery, observed : 'All the signs are that we shall
have trouble from him very soon.'

In contrast with Sir Winston's measured, majestic de-
livery, Mr Morrison's style is light and conversational. Sir
Winston in 1940 called upon the nation :

'Let us . . . brace ourselves to our duties, and so bear ourselves that, if the British Empire and its Commonwealth last
for a thousand years, men will say: "This was their finest
hour."'

Mr Morrison's famous wartime slogan was : 'Go to it.'

He is not known for his polished epigrams or witty asides
and is apt to overwork words like 'nice and tidy' or

'naughty'. Yet he is a formidable adversary. He is expert at taking the wind out of an opponent's sails. He will present the other side's case with meticulous fairness, argument by argument, and then make it appear vaguely unreasonable, thus leaving his opponent the choice of either of repeating arguments which the House has already heard, or of saying nothing.

And he loves a scrap. Whenever one of his Party's former junior Ministers, like Mr Woodrow Wyatt, runs into trouble with Sir Winston, he usually rushes in to retrieve the situation or at least to cover the retreat.

Sir Winston once called Herbert Morrison, the politician, 'a curious mixture of geniality and venom'. Mr Morrison would probably claim that Sir Winston's treatment of him in the House is compounded of ingredients which do not seem very dissimilar.

In a debate on Civil Defence, some Labour Members had urged the Government to transfer responsibility for Civil Defence from the Home Office to the Ministry of Defence. Sir Winston had just refused when Mr Morrison unexpectedly intervened.

MR H. MORRISON [Labour]: *Is the right hon. Gentleman aware that, as one who experienced this office, in the wartime Government of which he was Prime Minister, I am quite sure he is right? I would urge him to stand firm upon the point.*

THE PRIME MINISTER: *I assure the right hon. Gentleman – I almost said my right hon. Friend, as he was in those days – I shall stand firm as a rock.*

[*Hansard,* 29 *Jan.* 1954, *col.* 1611]

Mr Morrison pressed Sir Winston to reveal the amount of money that would be saved by the amalgamation of two Government departments, but Sir Winston refused to give exact figures.

MR H. MORRISON [Labour]: . . . *surely it is elementary that when the Government consider these matters they have the figure of the immediate economies before them? I have handled some of these things, and that is always known . . .*
THE PRIME MINISTER: *The right hon. Gentleman said that he had considerable experience of these kinds of things, but he means considerable experience of these kinds of things the other way round: namely, that he would rapidly multiply and expand Departments in all directions and cast away our scanty store, in the hopes of successful electioneering.*
                          [*Hansard, 2 March 1953, col. 39*]

Mr Woodrow Wyatt, a junior Minister at the War Office in the Labour Government, had challenged Sir Winston's attitude on Britain's links with the European Army, and Mr Morrison eventually intervened in the exchanges that followed.

MR WOODROW WYATT [Labour]: *Is he aware that the French have a strong feeling that he himself has badly let them down, because he made a great many promises before he became Prime Minister about the co-operation which we would have with the European Army, all of which he has broken? Does he not realize that the European Defence Community will founder completely unless we make a better gesture than we have so far made to the French?*
THE PRIME MINISTER: *I am sure that questions, including supplementary questions, should be asked primarily for the purpose of gaining information and not for self-advertisement.*

Mr Wyatt: *Is the Prime Minister not aware that as he never gives us any information it is sometimes necessary to give him some information in order to jolt him out of his apathy?*

Mr Noel-Baker [Labour]: *Since the Prime Minister is presumably proposing to the French that we should undertake obligations towards the E.D.C. and since that is a matter on which this House must ultimately decide, would it not be an advantage that we should now have the information about what the Government propose?*

The Prime Minister: *I said in my speech on Monday week all that I think it necessary or desirable to say at the present moment.*

Mr H. Morrison [Labour]: *Does the Prime Minister remember the occasion in Strasbourg – I remember it, as I was there – when he made his great speech about a European Army? Does he think the spirit and text of that speech is consistent with the policy being followed by him as Prime Minister? Does he not remember also that when he was in opposition he used Question Time for his own advertisement as much as anybody else?*

The Prime Minister: *I am sure that the last part of the right hon. Gentleman's supplementary question which gave him the opportunity of indulging in the art of* tu quoque *was the only part to which he really attached importance.*

[*Hansard, 20 May 1953, col. 2080*]

The Opposition were trying to force Sir Winston into admitting that his refusal to develop more formal political links within the Commonwealth was inconsistent with the policy of close political union he had advocated for Europe.

'Pedagogue turned politician'

MR H. MORRISON [Labour]: *Are we to take it that the right hon. Gentleman is opposed to the principle of federalism in relation to the Commonwealth but is in favour of it so far as Western Europe is concerned?*

THE PRIME MINISTER: *I do not myself conceive that federalism is immediately possible within the Commonwealth. I have never been in favour of it in Europe and I am astonished that the right hon. Gentleman, when he visited Strasbourg and was such a distinguished success there, did not notice some of the fundamental facts.* [*Hansard, 8 July* 1952, *col.* 1093]

In a debate on the Government's general policy, Mr Morrison was trying to shake Sir Winston out of his benign, conciliatory mood.

MR H. MORRISON [Labour]: *At the end of the war, he got very cross with some of us when we broke up the Coalition.*

THE PRIME MINISTER *indicated assent.*

MR MORRISON: *He got very cross with me in particular. The right hon. Gentleman came down to Lewisham and said there was one man whom he never wanted to see again.*

THE PRIME MINISTER: *I have got over that.*

MR MORRISON: *What can you do with the right hon. Gentleman?*   [*Hansard, 4 Nov.* 1953, *col.* 171]

MR HUGH GAITSKELL

A novel phenomenon at Westminster since the war has been the pedagogue turned politician. Few dons whom the post-war stampede from the universities swept into Parliament have undergone that transformation more successfully than Mr Gaitskell.

A product of Winchester and New College, Oxford, a lecturer in political economy at the University of London and for the Workers' Educational Association until 1939, and a temporary civil servant at the Ministry of Economic Warfare under Dr Dalton during the war, he did not enter Parliament until 1945. Five years, later, in 1950, he was Chancellor of the Exchequer, and the political pundits seriously began to think of him as a future Socialist Prime Minister.

Yet so rapid has been his rise that the didactic manner of the lecture room still clings to him. In 1947, when he was Minister of Fuel and Power, he urged the nation to have fewer baths, as a measure of saving coal. 'I have never had a great many baths myself,' he explained to a meeting at Hastings, 'and I can assure those who have them as a habit that it does not make much difference to their health if they have fewer.'

It was a piece of advice which Sir Winston did not allow to pass without comment. 'When Ministers of the Crown speak like this on behalf of His Majesty's Government, the Prime Minister and his friends have no need to wonder why they are getting increasingly into bad odour. I had even asked myself, when meditating on these points, whether you, Mr Speaker, would admit the word 'lousy' as a Parliamentary expression in referring to the Administration, provided of course it was not intended in a contemptuous sense but purely as one of factual narration.'

Mr Gaitskell's tenure at the Ministry of Fuel was not a period of undiluted delight for him. He never seemed entirely at ease, grappling with the problems of the newly nationalized industries, and it was with obvious relief that he transferred to the Treasury and the complexities of the dollar gap.

But even there his happiness was not complete. For Sir Winston had declared war on the Socialist Government's economic terminology. Why use 'disinflation' for 'deflation', he asked. Why not 'non-undisinflation'? And what was all this jargon about 'the infrastructure of a supranational authority'? The only explanation he could think of was that the words 'infra' and 'supra' had been introduced 'by the band of intellectual highbrows who are naturally anxious to impress British labour with the fact that they learned Latin at Winchester.'

And during one of Mr Gaitskell's speeches on economic affairs he left the House of Commons in no doubt that he, for one, was not fascinated by figures. Mr Gaitskell was busy marshalling his facts, and the House was following his performance with interest, when Sir Winston suddenly sat up and looked about with a distracted air. He went through his pockets, looked down at his feet and carefully examined the floor. At first only a few Members noticed what he was doing, but soon the whole House, even the public in the Galleries, was craning in his direction. Mr Gaitskell hesitated and then stopped, the thread of his argument broken beyond repair. He had 'lost' the House.

Sir Winston seemed to be blissfully unaware of what had happened until he looked up to find everyone's eyes upon him. He glanced across at Mr Gaitskell and was heard to mutter by way of explanation, 'I was only looking for my jujube.' *The Scotsman* reported the incident on the following day under the headline 'The Fall of the Pastille'.

Mr Gaitskell was first 'discovered' by Dr Dalton, who, as the Labour Party's unofficial talent scout, has launched many a promising young man into politics. He soon attracted the attention of the late Sir Stafford Cripps and climbed the political ladder under the 'Iron Chancellor's' powerful protection. His financial orthodoxy, however, did not endear him to Mr Bevan. The two quarrelled bitterly over the charges on artificial teeth and spectacles which Gaitskell introduced in his Budget in 1951, and eventually Bevan resigned from the Labour Government. Since then Gaitskell has been as strenuously devoted to holding all the orthodox Labour views as Bevan to demolishing them.

Today Mr Gaitskell is the hope of the anti-Bevanites. In their view he is the obvious successor to Mr Attlee and Mr Morrison. His relentless grasp of complex details and his gift of lucid exposition have won him admiration far beyond his own party. Mr Butler, his opposite number on the Conservative side, is known to respect his ability deeply, and in the House the two frequently exchange the sort of private little jokes which are incomprehensible to all but Chancellors of the Exchequer and Financial Secretaries of the Treasury.

Sir Winston, however, is not on record as ever having spoken a complimentary word about him.

In a debate on the economic position of the country, Mr Gaitskell had delivered a sustained attack on the Conservative Government's economic policies, and it was Sir Winston's turn to reply.

THE PRIME MINISTER: *I was surprised to see the right hon. Gentleman the Member for Leeds, South [Mr Gaitskell], standing so smiling and carefree at the Despatch Box as if he had no responsibility for the shocking and shameful state to which our finances were reduced during his tenure of the Exchequer. When a Minister has in a single year brought his country from the best position it had held since the war to the verge of bankruptcy, and when he has left to his successors heart-tearing problems to face and solve, I wonder indeed that*

he should find nothing to do but mock and jeer at the efforts
that others make to clear up the confusion and disorder that he
left behind him. Indeed, I almost think it is a pity that he ever
escaped from Winchester. [Hansard, 30 July 1952, col. 1512]

Sir Winston was in the middle of one of his extensive surveys of the defence situation which he periodically gives the
House.

THE PRIME MINISTER: *I must now warn the House that I*
am going to make an unusual departure. I am going to make a
Latin quotation. It is one which I hope will not offend the
detachment of the old school tie . . . The quotation is, Arma
virumque cano, *which, for the benefit of our Winchester*
friends, I may translate as 'Arms and the men I sing'. That
generally describes my theme.
MR HUGH GAITSKELL [Labour]: *Should it not be*
'man', the singular instead of the plural?
THE PRIME MINISTER: *Little did I expect that I should*
receive assistance on a classical matter from such a quarter.
                    [Hansard, 5 March 1953, col. 577]

While the House of Commons was debating the Budget,
which always takes several days, Sir Winston, stung by Mr
Gaitskell's criticisms of his Government's Budget, had made
a vigorous personal attack on Mr Gaitskell and his political
mentor, Dr Dalton, in a speech at Glasgow. Dr Dalton, who
had served as Chancellor of the Exchequer in the Labour
Government from 1945 until his resignation in 1947, availed
himself of the Budget debate to reply to these charges.

MR HUGH DALTON [Labour]: *I am much obliged to the*
Prime Minister for listening to some of what I have to say.
We now return to our public duty of debunking this Budget.

This work was well begun by my right hon. Friend the Member for Leeds, South [Mr Gaitskell], last Wednesday – so well begun that he obviously got under the Prime Minister's skin, as a speech made by the Prime Minister in Glasgow on Friday shows. The Prime Minister used these words of my right hon. Friend: ' This old-school-tie careerist –'

THE PRIME MINISTER: *It was not correctly reported. I said, ' This old-school-tie left-wing careerist.'*

MR DALTON: *That amendment will be helpful to emphasize a comment I shall make in a moment. ' This old-school-tie left-wing careerist may rightly claim to have been the worst Chancellor since Mr Dalton.' I could not let these words slip past unnoticed today . . . In these days we tend to be too polite in political exchanges and I welcome the robust and straightforward abuse from the Prime Minister, hoping he will not resent counter-attack. ' The worst Chancellor since Mr Dalton' – that may be a matter for argument.*

THE PRIME MINISTER: *May I assure the right hon. Gentleman that I did not attempt in any way to set myself up as a judge of the competition between himself and the right hon. Gentleman?* [Hansard, 20 April 1953, col. 652]

Churchill v. Bevan

Before the First World War the young Churchill's partner-
ship with Lloyd George kept the political pot boiling over
merrily. In the 1950's it has been the political antagonism of
a Churchill, approaching his eightieth year, towards another
Welshman, twenty-three years his junior, that has kept the
House of Commons on its toes.

In his time Sir Winston has called Mr Bevan 'the latest
Welsh product', a 'Merchant of Discourtesy', a 'Minister of
Disease' in need of 'psychiatrical treatment' and in a flash
of Olympian anger 'a squalid nuisance'. And Mr Bevan has
retaliated by dubbing Sir Winston 'the entertainer of the
House of Commons', 'the bogy man of the country', and 'a
political chameleon'.

Yet when the House of Commons met for the first time after Sir Winston's election victory in 1951, M.P.s were treated to a rare spectacle. Behind Mr Speaker's Chair they could see the Prime Minister and Mr Bevan in apparently amicable conversation. No one could hear what they were saying, but as they parted, they bowed to one another with elaborate courtesy.

And shortly afterwards the newly appointed Prime Minister entered the Chamber – on the wrong side of the House, on the Opposition side. M.P.s were stunned as he made his way to the seat he had occupied for the previous six years as Leader of the Opposition. Had he forgotten his recent election victory? Had Mr Bevan's charm and golden tongue succeeded in a few seconds where half a century of Socialist arguments had failed to make the slightest impression? Labour M.P.s burst into cheers, happy to claim him for their own at last. Surprised, Sir Winston surveyed first the Labour benches and then his own startled followers on the other side of the House. Less than half a dozen steps would have taken him across the floor of the Chamber to his Conservative colleagues on the Treasury Bench. But Sir Winston refused to do the obvious. Without saying a word, he turned and slowly walked out of the House again, to reappear a little later – on the right side of the House. This time the Conservatives welcomed him like a conquering hero.

Trying to fathom the enigma of how Sir Winston feels about Mr Bevan has long been a favourite parlour game at Westminster.

In the House of Commons, as in any other Club, Members are held in esteem not for the colour of their politics, but for their personalities, and Winston Churchill is himself far too colourful a figure not to be intrigued by Aneurin Bevan. He likes a fighter and appreciates a good Parliamentary performance with all the enjoyment of the connoisseur. He is usually in his seat when the Socialist ex-miner makes a big speech, and when Mr Bevan was Minister of Labour, he even interrupted on one occasion just as 'the most mischievous mouth in wartime' seemed on the point of launching a scathing attack on him, to say with a smile: 'Don't spoil a good speech now.' And, returning the smile, Bevan took the hint.

Nowadays Sir Winston occasionally seeks out the Welshman in the lobbies and, while lesser mortals stand back and wonder what is going to happen next, wishes him a Merry Christmas, or a good and fruitful trip if Mr Bevan should be about to leave for foreign parts. It can be interpreted to mean a lot – or nothing, and Sir Winston, one suspects, takes a mischievous delight in sending Westminster into a flurry of rumour and speculation.

'Nye' Bevan and Winston Churchill first met socially in the early thirties. Bevan at that time was sharing a flat with Frank Owen, who was then a Liberal M.P. and later became editor of Lord Beaverbrook's *Evening Standard* and Lord Rothermere's *Daily Mail*. He had fashionable London at his feet. Mayfair hostesses showered him with invitations, and his zest for good living, combined with his fiery politics, earned him the title of 'the Bollinger Bolshevik'.

There is a story that in the late thirties when Churchill was vainly trying to open the Chamberlain Government's eyes to the German danger, and Bevan was running into trouble with his own party for his efforts in organizing an anti-Fascist 'Popular Front', Churchill one evening proposed across the dinner table that they should join forces and form a two-man rebel party in the House of Commons.

It is fascinating to speculate what would have happened if they had. But it is unlikely that their party would have survived very long. For, while they may agree on food and wine, their politics have nothing in common.

Their duels during the war reached a pitch of bitterness that at times staggered the House. There was no touch of humour, no trace of wit in their exchanges, and on one occasion the late Miss Eleanor Rathbone, one of the University Members, intervened to say that 'nobody who has watched Mr Bevan and his evolutions in this House can doubt that he entertains a malicious and virulent dislike of the Prime Minister'.

Towards the end of the war Sir Winston's humour gradually reasserted itself. Mr Bevan at that time was persistently pressing for information about the alleged installation of 'reactionary' governments in the liberated countries, and in answer to one of those questions Sir Winston replied blandly : 'I should think it hardly possible to state the opposite of the truth with more precision.' Aneurin Bevan, however, is not the man to be squashed by a neat reply. As Minister of Health in Mr Attlee's Cabinet he continued to send the political temperature up to boiling-point at regular intervals. He called the Tories 'lower than vermin', the British Press 'the most prostituted in the world', and after his sensational resignation from the Labour Government early in 1951, even his erstwhile Cabinet colleagues, Gaitskell, Morrison and Shinwell, felt the lash of his tongue.

Sir Winston's reaction depends in each case on the target at which Mr Bevan is aiming. If it is the Conservative Party or Government, Sir Winston joins issue immediately. There is a head-on clash, and M.P.s thrill once again to the glory of having causes to fight for, heroes to champion and villains to hiss. Forgotten are the worthy but genteel exchanges between Mr Butler and Mr Gaitskell about the finer points of Britain's trade balances, forgotten, too, the long and dreary hours of committee work, the lack of secretarial help and the worry of making ends meet on an M.P.'s salary. The fight is on, the air is charged, and everyone feels happier.

If Mr Bevan's target, however, is the orthodox wing of his own Party – or at least, can be made to appear so – then Sir Winston is at pains to give himself the air of a nervous bystander, unwittingly caught in a dog fight. Cross-questioned once by Shinwell and Bevan, he turned to the Speaker with a show of helplessness and asked the Chair to decide which of 'the two right honourable competitors' he should reply to first. His solicitous concern for the Labour Party's difficulties knows no bounds, and he looks kindness itself as he judiciously drops a few grains of salt into the open wound and suggests to a Bevanite or anti-Bevanite that he should not question the Government but discuss the matter amicably with his colleagues in his own Party.

Of all the prominent Labour Members in the House Mr Bevan seems to be worried the least by these tactics. He does not seem to mind swimming against the stream. He wants more Socialism and less talk of consolidation. He is against German rearmament, Western interference in Asia and too much dependence on the White House and the State Department. He lives by defence through attack. His command of language is second only to Sir Winston's, and even those who detest him cannot resist the spell of his colourful imagery. In 1943 he was not alone in attacking Allied strategy in Italy, but his description of the Allied Command approaching the conquest of Italy, 'like an old man approaching a young bride – fascinated, sluggish, apprehensive', is still remembered.

Yet somehow Sir Winston usually contrives to have the last word. And frequently it is the older man who provokes a tussle for sheer love of a good fight.

'Persistently pressing
for information'

There is one subject, however, on which Sir Winston is not expected to make a pronouncement – Mr Bevan's prospects of becoming Prime Minister. Indeed, it is unlikely that he has given the matter much thought, except possibly as a topic of conversation with Gaitskell or Shinwell.

Sir Winston's comments on Mr Bevan frequently come in the most unexpected circumstances, as when he was speaking on the recognition of Communist China.

THE PRIME MINISTER: *As we had great interests there, and also on general grounds, I thought that it would be a good thing to have diplomatic representation. But if you recognize anyone it does not mean that you like him. We all, for instance, recognize the right hon. Gentleman the Member for Ebbw Vale [Mr Bevan].*

[*Hansard*, 1 July 1952, col. 288]

Their differences on foreign affairs are the cause of many brushes in the House. Mr Eden had made a statement that British and United States policy in the Far East would be marked by increasing harmony.

MR BEVAN [Labour]: *Being a Welshman, I am interested in the structure of harmony. 'Increasing harmony' means being of increasing accord. The Foreign Secretary made it quite clear . . . that there were deep differences of opinion between Great Britain and the United States on China policy. Are we moving towards them, or are they moving towards us? From what situation does the harmony arise? I wish the Prime Minister would listen, because he will not hear as much good sense from the Chief Whip as I am giving him.*

THE PRIME MINISTER: *I apologize to the right hon. Gentleman. I am afraid I did not hear what he said. I am so sorry to have missed it. Would he mind repeating it?*

MR BEVAN: *It was not a good enough joke to repeat . . .*
[*Hansard*, 26 Feb. 1952, col. 994]

In the course of a debate on the denationalization of road transport Sir Winston was making it clear that the Government were determined to go ahead with their measure, irrespective of the Labour Party's opposition.

THE PRIME MINISTER: *We are not trying to make party strife bitter.*

HON. MEMBERS: *Oh.*

THE PRIME MINISTER: *We are not trying to prepare for an election or anything of that kind, as the right hon. Member for Ebbw Vale [Mr Bevan] is writing in his newspaper, quivering with fear. We are very anxious to carry matters forward —*

MR BEVAN *rose —*

HON. MEMBERS: *Sit down.*

THE PRIME MINISTER: *The right hon. Gentleman can quiver after I sit down.* [*Hansard*, 23 April 1953, col. 1587]

An article by Mr Bevan on the subject of Anglo-Egyptian relations, which had been published in one of General Neguib's newspapers in Cairo, aroused much adverse comment. Defending his action, Mr Bevan blamed the Conservative

Press in general and Lord Beaverbrook's *Daily Express* in particular for the furore his article had caused in Britain.

MR BEVAN [Labour]: *The only reason why the attack was made was because the article was published in Cairo and because Conservative newspapers wanted some means of diverting public attention from the revolution in the Conservative ranks. It is not the first time that this has happened . . . The 'Daily Express', the newspaper whose proprietor is so friendly with the right hon. Gentleman the Prime Minister –*
THE PRIME MINISTER: *I think I first met the right hon. Gentleman at his house.* [Hansard, 17 Dec. 1953, col. 604]

To the charge that he should not have published articles abroad criticizing the British Government at a time when it was engaged in delicate negotiations, Mr Bevan recalled first Sir Winston's articles in the foreign press attacking the Baldwin and Chamberlain Governments and then Lord Randolph Churchill's attacks on British policy in Egypt in the last century.

MR BEVAN [Labour]: *This criticism of his father against British policy in Egypt was uttered when there was fighting in Egypt.*
THE PRIME MINISTER: *The right hon. Gentleman has hitherto been trying to hide behind me. Now I gather he is endeavouring to hide behind my father. I am sure we can both take care of ourselves.* [Hansard, 17 Dec. 1953, col. 610]

Sir Winston was reviewing the progress of the rearmament programme and allowed himself to make a few comments on aspects of the programme on which the Bevanites and the rest of the Labour Party did not see eye to eye.

THE PRIME MINISTER: *Some of the late Government's programme must necessarily roll forward into a future year. This point was, I believe, made by the right hon. Gentleman the Member for Ebbw Vale [Mr Bevan] after his resignation. I do not reproach the late Government on this score. They tried their best* . . .

MR BEVAN [Labour]: *Will the right hon. Gentleman give way?* . . . *Am I* . . . *to understand that the Government has abandoned the three-year period and has added some unknown period to the length of the rearmament programme?*

THE PRIME MINISTER: *As events develop, the right hon. Gentleman will no doubt watch them with attention, and the discussions which, from time to time, he will have with his former colleagues will no doubt be both instructive and animated on both sides.*

HON. MEMBERS: *Answer.*

THE PRIME MINISTER: *I am not really wishing to embark on a debate with the right hon. Gentleman. I was giving him an honourable mention in despatches for having, by accident* –

MR BEVAN *rose.*

MR DEPUTY SPEAKER [Col. Sir Charles MacAndrew]: *If the Prime Minister does not give way, hon. and right hon. Gentlemen must resume their seats.*

THE PRIME MINISTER: *I will give way in a moment. I was giving the right hon. Gentleman an honourable mention for having, it appears by accident, perhaps not from the best motives, happened to be right.*

[*Hansard, 6 Dec. 1951, col. 2611*]

When Sir Winston announced that the number of Labour Attachés at British embassies was to be reduced, he provoked a storm of protests from the Socialist benches.

MR NOEL-BAKER [Labour]: *Does he not agree that this is a particularly bad time to do anything that will weaken the solidarity of the democratic forces in the world?*

THE PRIME MINISTER: *I think that democratic solidarity throughout the world will not be affected by there being 17 Labour Attachés instead of 20.*

MR BEVAN: *Is the right hon. Gentleman aware that every Minister of Labour since the war, including the late Ernest Bevin, attached very great importance to these officers, and that in this disturbed condition of the world today it is a very serious thing indeed to cut us off from the sources of information which these Labour Attachés were able to obtain? Are there not other ways of reducing the establishments abroad without reducing the one single element that is beginning to alleviate the caste system in the legations?*

THE PRIME MINISTER: *I am naturally interested to see the right hon. Gentleman in his place, but I cannot feel that the question he has asked adds anything to the pith of our discussion.*   [Hansard, 26 Nov. 1952, col. 455]

During a debate on the denationalization of road transport, Mr Bevan was raking the Government benches with his fire, attacking the Prime Minister, the Minister of Education, Miss Horsbrugh, whose funds had just been cut, and other Conservatives, as they aroused his displeasure, while Sir Winston sat opposite him on the Treasury Bench, waiting for an opening.

MR BEVAN [Labour]: *I do not agree . . . that the right hon. Gentleman [the Prime Minister] is a good Parliamentarian. He never was. He never used the House of Commons for anything at all except to come down to now and again and make exhortations or use it as an audience . . . I do not know what the right hon. Lady the Minister of Education [Miss Florence Horsbrugh] is grinning at. I was told by one of my hon. Friends this afternoon that that is a face which has sunk a thousand scholarships . . . The hon. and gallant Member for Knutsford [Lt.-Col. Bromley Davenport] makes grimaces. Nature has already been sufficiently unkind to him.*

LT.-COL. BROMLEY DAVENPORT [Conservative]: *I was grimacing with pain because I could not bear the appearance of the right hon. Gentleman at such close quarters.*

THE PRIME MINISTER: *You must make allowances for people that are 'lower than vermin'.*

[*Hansard*, 23 April 1953, col. 1587]

Shortly before Parliament rose for its summer recess in 1954, Mr Bevan, who was about to leave for China as a member of an official Labour Party delegation, asked the Prime Minister to tell the House before the holidays what reply the Government proposed to send to a recent Soviet Note suggesting a general European Security Pact.

THE PRIME MINISTER: *I cannot guarantee that the complexities of the situation will be cleared away within the next few days. The proposal which has been made by the Soviet Government raises important questions connected with conferences, all of which must be discussed between the three allies.*

MR BEVAN: *Would it not be extremely undesirable for the House to disperse for the Summer Recess without knowing what the answer will be on a matter of this sort?*

THE PRIME MINISTER: *The House does disperse at different seasons of the year, and I understood that the right hon. Gentleman himself had made his plans for distant journeys. We should not wish to interfere with them.*

[*Hansard*, 27 July 1954, col. 232]

Obiter Dicta

Before the war the Stock Exchange was generally held to be the source of bar and cocktail party humour. Latterly, however, it has suffered a notable decline and for some years now it has been the fashion for anyone wishing to be smart to quote Sir Winston Churchill. The result has been that a large currency of stories is in circulation of which not a few are counterfeit. The only authority who can certainly tell the genuine from the false is Sir Winston Churchill himself because, at least, the standard of stories or remarks attributed to him has been high.

It was quite obvious that, after 1945, many of Winston Churchill's barbs would be directed against the Socialist party. He had, of course, started to work on the Socialists much earlier. At the outset of his career he had stated, 'They are not fit to manage a whelk stall.' And, in turn, he pilloried them as a 'government of the duds, by the duds, and for the duds', and a form of Government that would vanish, 'unwept, unhonoured, unsung and unhung'.

After 1945, during the period of shortages and controls, his evident dislike of the theory and of many of the leading personalities of Socialism produced a crop of sallies. Mr Attlee came first. The casual remark, 'Attlee is a very modest man', evoked the terse rejoinder, 'And with reason.' On another occasion the Socialist leader was pilloried as 'a sheep in wolf's clothing'. At least, that is how the remark is authoritatively quoted. There is a variation which insists on a 'sheep in sheep's clothing', but it is doubtful if Winston Churchill ever uttered either.

There is no such doubt about his assaults upon the austere Chancellor of the Exchequer, Sir Stafford Cripps. Cripps, all brain and with little apparent humanity, was always anathema to Churchill. It is this type of politician which Winston Churchill objects to most and he lambasted him in a speech in the House in 1946.

'Neither of his colleagues can compare with him in that acuteness and energy of mind with which he devotes himself to so many topics injurious to the strength and welfare of the State.'

In addition to this he on several occasions has got muddled with the name – in a slightly unfortunate way. Whether or not Churchill was the author of the remark about Cripps, 'There, but for the Grace of God, goes God' – has never been properly established.

During the first session of the Council of Europe at Strasbourg in 1949 Winston Churchill attended for some days as a British representative. The Socialists sent Mr Herbert Morrison, then Lord President of the Council and Deputy Prime Minister, to watch him. Churchill's progress was triumphant – he was acclaimed in the city by cheering crowds, he wept, he spoke in French and gave wisdom and guidance to the Council. In retaliation all Morrison could do was to raise questions about the source of Winston Churchill's foreign currency. The row raged for some days until Herbert Morrison approached Churchill in the corridors of the University building. 'Is this a question of money?' demanded Churchill. 'Then you know what you can do with it.'

The next year at Strasbourg it was the turn of the Heepish Doctor Dalton, whose talent for indiscretion had previously forced him to resign as Chancellor of the Exchequer. In the Assembly he leaned across to comment on the seating arrangement which had caused him to be sitting close to Churchill.

'I see we're divided only by one Italian,' he purred.

'That's not all that divides us,' grunted Churchill.

But his shafts have not been restricted to the opposite side. Many years ago when Sir Alfred Bossom first entered the House of Commons as a Conservative Member, Churchill turned to ask who he was. On being told, he snorted: 'Bossom? Bossom? It's neither one thing nor the other.'

When he was in Opposition after the war Winston Churchill used to spend a good deal of time in the Smoking Room of the House. This is a dark, club-like room with leather armchairs, looking out on the Terrace. In the past, drinks were served there as long as Members required them, which was frequently all night. Now that has been stopped, but you may still have a drink from the bar in the corner until half an hour after the House has risen. Sir Winston (who was once inadvertently and inaccurately referred to by an American as 'Sir Ginston') normally drinks brandy. He enjoys alcohol and makes no secret of the fact. He once referred to it as 'the ineradicable habit of a lifetime' and of it he made an excellent aphorism.

'I have taken more out of alcohol than alcohol has taken out of me.'

Of all his famous 'asides' the best known is the one he is credited with making after his famous speech 'We shall fight on the beaches'. Having delivered this stirring defiance in a way that none who heard it will ever forget, he is said to have covered the microphone with his hand and added: 'We will hit 'em over the head with beer bottles, which is all we have to fight with.'

But his best quips have been saved for the House, where they are accurately reported. And for his enemies, who do well to forget them promptly. Not long after the war the Labour Government had introduced a formidable programme of legislation. As August drew near overworked M.P.s, especially the Socialists, pressed Herbert Morrison, the Deputy Prime Minister, to state when the Parliamentary Recess would begin. The Leader of the Opposition rose to his feet gravely. 'We are all very anxious for Labour Members to get away in time for the grouse shooting.'

MR CALLAGHAN

MR WYATT

Among the Minnows

Emrys Hughes has established himself as a regular and persistent questioner of the Prime Minister. Anything connected with napalm, atomic or hydrogen bombs, with the black races and aborigines, or American bombers stationed in Britain, will automatically bring him to his feet. It is doubtful if Senator McCarthy would approve of Emrys Hughes, but he is far from being 'a bleeding heart of the extreme Left wing'. Like another Parliamentary revolutionary, 'Jimmy' Maxton, Hughes is rather a benign man.

He is a Welshman who married a daughter of the pioneer Socialist, the late Keir Hardie. He is also a journalist who has travelled in Russia. The force which drives him appears to be humanitarian and Sir Winston Churchill reserves for him a special type of answer which would, at times, even indicate a certain affection.

On a question by Mr Emrys Hughes on Civil List expen-
diture and Churchill's reduction of Cabinet Ministers' salaries, the Prime Minister was not unforgetful that Hughes is
the son of a former Tonypandy minister.

MR HUGHES [Labour]: *Owing to the popularity the Government has gained by the reduction of their salaries, is not the
Prime Minister prepared to apply the principle to the big item
of more than £500,000 spent on the Civil List?*
THE PRIME MINISTER: *Dim o gwbl. (Nothing at all.)*
                            [*Hansard, 12 Nov. 1951, col. 648*]

On Home Guard recruitment. (Churchill was at that time
not only Prime Minister, but also Minister of Defence.)

MR HUGHES: *Is the right hon. Gentleman aware that the
Minister of Defence was absent from the first Home Guard
Parade last night? Is he now on open arrest awaiting Court
martial?*
THE PRIME MINISTER: *I was pursuing my studies into the
Welsh language.*   [*Hansard, 28 Nov. 1951, col. 1519*]

The Prime Minister continued his allusions to Hughes's
Welsh ancestry in the following year during a debate on
defence.

THE PRIME MINISTER: . . . *I would not use the word 'im-
prudently' if I had not long studied all the economic advan-
tages of the Cardwell system, with a battalion abroad and a
battalion at home, and an inter-flow of reserves and reinforce-
ments between them. These battalions now raised, in one of
which the hon. Member for Ayrshire, South [Mr Emrys
Hughes], took so much interest, the Black – what was it?*
MR HUGHES: *The Black Watch.*

THE PRIME MINISTER: *I thought it was the 'Black Welsh'.*   [*Hansard,* 5 *March* 1952, *col.* 436]

On a question upon atom bomb tests in Australia, initiated by the Labour Government:

MR EMRYS HUGHES [Labour]: *Is the Prime Minister aware that the Australian aborigines who are converted to Christianity are now thinking of sending missionaries to this country, because they think that the atom bomb can only have been invented by savages and barbarians?*
THE PRIME MINISTER: *I hope that the Leader of the Opposition will not feel unduly hurt.*
[*Hansard,* 1 *May* 1952, *col.* 1673]

During another exchange on atomic weapon tests in Australia, Mr Emrys Hughes asked the Prime Minister to what extent the safety of bird and animal life has been considered in relation to the atomic weapon tests that were to be carried out at the Montebello Islands, off Australia.

THE PRIME MINISTER: *The report of a recent special survey showing that there is very little animal or bird life on the Montebello Islands was one of the factors in the choice of the site for the test of the United Kingdom atomic weapon.*
I should add, however, that an expedition which went to the islands 50 years ago reported that giant rats, wild cats and wallabies were seen, and these may have caused the hon. Member some anxiety. However, the officer who explored the islands recently says that he found only some lizards, two sea eagles and what looked like a canary sitting on a perch.
MR HUGHES [Labour]: *Will the Prime Minister tell us whether any competent officer will go on this expedition? Is he aware that there are still civilized people in this country*

who are interested in bird and animal life? Will he get some
report which will satisfy civilized human beings that no un-
necessary destruction of wild life will take place?
THE PRIME MINISTER: *Certainly. I think everything*
should be done to avoid the destruction of bird life and animal
life and also of human life.

[Hansard, 21 May 1952, col. 472]

MR WOODROW WYATT

Of all those who attempt to harry Sir Winston Churchill
with earnest and persistent questions perhaps the busiest is
Mr Woodrow Wyatt. Time and again a dark, bespectacled
face is projected across the back of the Opposition Front
Bench in the direction of Despatch Box and Prime Minister.
The questions are usually upon military affairs, which is not
odd, in one sense, because in 1944 Woodrow Wyatt rose to
the rank of major in the Army and, like at least one of his
colleagues, a comparatively lowly service rank was the fore-
runner of higher political rating. Wyatt was a Junior Minister as Financial Secretary to the War Office in 1951. The
military spirit and thunder of arms, however, sit uneasily
upon his shoulders. Although many majors looked like him
during the war, Wyatt is more of a literary character in appearance. He has been on the editorial staff of the *New*
Statesman and Nation and of Bevan's *Tribune*; he is also founder and editor of the highbrow and rather dreary collection
of short stories called *English Story*. He has written two
books but, all in all, it would seem that in his case the pen has
been as least as unprofitable as the sword.

Sir Winston Churchill's attitude to him can best be described as Olympian. He once looked over his spectacles in
Wyatt's direction and inquired 'Still alive?' But Wyatt is,

very much so, and hopping. He appears to consider that the repeated publicity he obtains in the newspapers from questions addressed to the Prime Minister is worth the drubbing he repeatedly gets.

On a question asking whether the Prime Minister would set up a Royal Commission to review the age limits for retirement throughout the public service:

MR WYATT [Labour]: *Is not the right hon. Gentleman aware that there is grave public disquiet that his right hon. Friend the Minister of Housing and Local Government should have given Lord Beveridge a year's notice to quit on the ground that he is 73 years of age, when there are older persons who are occupying even more responsible positions? Is it not time that the question of the relation between the age of a person and his capacity to do his job should be reviewed in the light of the discoveries of medical science?*

THE PRIME MINISTER: *This Question, although it may be prompted by the hon. Member's own ambitions, is nevertheless one which has always been decided hitherto in accordance with the opinions of a majority in the House of Commons.* [*Hansard, 18 June 1952, col. 1201*]

On the Mediterranean Naval command:

MR WYATT [Labour]: *Is it not a fact that in the Atlantic Command British ships are under the command of the American Supreme Allied Commander, and why should not the right hon. Gentleman insist on the same arrangement for American ships in the Mediterranean to be under the command of the British Supreme Allied Commander; and is it not shameful that he should have agreed to an arrangement altogether much less than the arrangement which we have agreed on in the Atlantic?*

THE PRIME MINISTER: *I think that I will leave the hon. Gentleman, in regard to this important matter which I think is very satisfactory, to rest on the word 'shameful'.*

[*Hansard, 16 Dec. 1952, col. 1205*]

The European Army frequently excited Mr Wyatt's curiosity.

MR WYATT [Labour]: *Has the Prime Minister seen a report in ' The Times' today which makes it quite clear that the fate of the French Government, and indeed that of the European Army, depends upon the answers which his Government give to the French proposals for a closer association with the European Army? Will he not remember that he himself invented the idea of the European Army at Strasbourg and suggested that we should be a member of it? Will he not summon forth the imagination which caused him once to suggest union with the French nation?*

THE PRIME MINISTER: *The hon. Gentleman seems to be more desirous of imparting information than of receiving it. Anyhow I have nothing to give him.*

[*Hansard, 18 Feb. 1953, col. 1243*]

On the conduct of the Korean truce talks and the composition of the U.N. delegation at Panmunjom:

MR WYATT [Labour]: *Has the Prime Minister seen, in regard to the actual conduct of the talks, a remarkable despatch in the ' Manchester Guardian' today, in which it is said quite clearly that unless some diplomats take part in the actual conduct of the truce talks, they are bound to collapse in a few weeks?*

THE PRIME MINISTER: *Was the hon. Gentleman the author of the despatch?* [*Hansard, 6 May 1953, col. 381*]

On the adoption of the new Belgian rifle for British forces :

MR WYATT [Labour] : *Is the Prime Minister aware that this announcement will prove a great discouragement to the brilliant British inventors who, over a long period, carefully invented and designed this new British rifle which, as the Prime Minister well knows, is undoubtedly the best that has ever been devised in the world? Is he aware that it is absolute nonsense to say that the Belgian rifle is equal to ours, since the weight of the round alone means that every rifleman will have to carry a greater burden into battle to be able to fire the same numbers of rounds? Is not this decision entirely due to the weakness of the Prime Minister in not standing up to the Americans for something which he knew was right?*

THE PRIME MINISTER: *I am quite ready that it should be attributed to me, and whether it is attributed by the hon. Gentleman to weakness or to wisdom I am entirely indifferent.*

[*Hansard,* 19 Jan. 1954, col. 835]

MR JAMES CALLAGHAN

James Callaghan is a young man with a round, ingenuous face and fluent speaking manner. He is a middle-of-the-road Socialist who has not suffered conspicuously from being a protégé of Dr Dalton. It is on record, however, that Dalton exclaimed to an American newspaperman at the Council of Europe at Strasbourg in 1950, 'That was a fine speech young Callaghan made!' to which he received the reply: 'Callaghan? Why, I never heard of him.'

Subsequently Callaghan became a junior Minister as Parliamentary and Financial Secretary to the Admiralty. He is thus in a position to call Admirals by their Christian names, which is always exciting for an ex-Lieutenant of the Royal

Naval Volunteer Reserve. It is this connection with the Navy which has probably at last made the Prime Minister recognize Callaghan – to the extent of continually putting this able, pushing young man into his place.

Indeed, the process started in the days when Callaghan was still a junior minister at the Admiralty.

MR CHURCHILL: . . . *We may have let our Navy down, but it can be revived. We have not let our Mercantile Marine diminish. On the contrary –*

MR CALLAGHAN [Labour] *rose –*

MR CHURCHILL: *The Parliamentary Secretary is a subordinate Minister of the Government and he should not interrupt from the Front Bench. We have not let our Mercantile Marine diminish. On the contrary, here are the figures.* [Interruption.] *I think I have the right to put forward the case for the potential contribution which Britain can make to war and transport on the seas. The United States have 12,400,000 tons of merchant shipping in use and 14 million tons in reserve. They have 250,000 tons under construction. Great Britain has 16,600,000 tons in use, or 19,600,000 tons if the Commonwealth and Empire are added, and two million tons under construction, some of it for foreign account. Moreover, we have far larger reserves of merchant –*

MR SNOW [Labour]: *Damned old fool.*

COLONEL GOMME-DUNCAN [Conservative]: *On a point of order. Is it in order for an hon. Member to refer to the right hon. Gentleman as 'a damned old fool'?*

THE CHAIRMAN: *It is certainly not in order.*

MR SNOW: *I beg to withdraw that statement and to apologize but, of course, the right hon. Gentleman has been extremely provocative.*

HON. MEMBERS: *Get out.*

MR CHURCHILL: *I always accept an apology here.*

MR SNOW: *Will not the right hon. Gentleman follow my example and apologize to my hon. Friend?*

MR IVOR OWEN THOMAS [Labour]: *May I call attention to the fact that this whole incident arose from –*

THE CHAIRMAN: *It was within the hearing of all Members of the Committee, and there is no point in calling attention to it now.*

MR THOMAS: *On a point of order. Is it in order for the right hon. Gentleman to refer to an hon. Member of the Committee as somewhat subordinate to another –* [Laughter.] *Let hon. Members wait for the whole of it – and, therefore, not entitled to the same consideration as a Member of the Government? Are not the rights of every Member on the Floor of the Committee equal?*

THE CHAIRMAN: *I do not think any procedural objection can be taken to the right hon. Gentleman's reference to the Parliamentary Secretary to the Admiralty.* [HON. MEMBERS: *Oh.*] *But it is, of course, true that the hon. Gentleman is the chief Minister of the Admiralty in the House.*

MR CHURCHILL: *Well, I understood that the Minister of Defence was going to take responsibility for the case today: and everything is relative in importance, and consequently, compared with the Minister of Defence, the hon. Gentleman must accept the position of being subordinate; although let me make it quite clear that this is the first time that I have ever heard the word 'subordinate' regarded as un-Parliamentary or even as almost an obscene expression. However, the 'damned old fool' has accepted the apology.*

[Hansard, 19 April 1951, col. 2035]

Later in the same debate Mr Shinwell attempted a score on this point.

MR SHINWELL [Labour]: . . . *I am not prepared to rely exclusively on the views expressed by him. There are other Members of the House who are subordinate to him, but who, nevertheless, are entitled to express an opinion.*
MR CHURCHILL: *Or insubordinate.*
[*Hansard, 19 April 1951, col.* 2077]

During Question Time Mr Callaghan, who played an obscure part at Strasbourg, led directly with his chin during questions on European affairs.

MR CALLAGHAN [Labour]: *Does not the Prime Minister remember the very powerful support he gave to this project when both he and I were at Strasbourg together, and he asked us why we were not appointing a Minister for European affairs?*
THE PRIME MINISTER: *I am sure I always look back with great pleasure to the occasions when I was at Strasbourg with the hon. Gentleman, but between forming these opinions of a favourable character and actually taking steps to create a new office there is a large gap, and in that gap all kinds of considerations have to be taken into account.*
[*Hansard, 28 April 1952, col.* 1025]

During questions on the responsibilities of Co-ordinating Ministers:

MR CALLAGHAN [Labour]: *My question is this, if I may repeat it for the Prime Minister: he has described to us that Lord Leathers exercises very important functions, but Lord Woolton says that his duties, on the other hand, are of a very minor character. May I ask how the Government reconcile those two things, and may I further ask the Prime Minister –*
THE PRIME MINISTER: *Try one at a time.*
[*Hansard, 6 May 1952, col.* 197]

During a debate on the British army and its adoption of the new Belgian rifle:

MR CALLAGHAN [Labour]: *Will the right hon. Gentleman –*
THE PRIME MINISTER: *I really did not know that the hon. Gentleman came into this. I saw the former Secretary of State for War, I saw the hon. Member for Aston [Mr Wyatt]; the leader of the Opposition has a great responsibility, and there is the late Minister of Defence. I thought that they would all have a claim to have a whack, but I do not see why, in a short debate like this, the hon. Gentleman cannot take his chance of rising when he is called.*   [Hansard, 1 Feb. 1954, col. 62]

Churchill v. Shinwell

It would be hard to imagine two men more unlike than Sir Winston Churchill and Emanuel Shinwell. On the one hand is the patrician statesman, scion of an illustrious family: on the other is the son of a clothing trader in the East End of London. Churchill's years of apprenticeship were spent in the army and as a precocious, but highly successful, foreign correspondent: ten years younger, Shinwell began in his father's workroom and in the hurly-burly of local politics in Glasgow.

Time decreed that both should end as Ministers and members of the Privy Council and, in Parliament, that Shinwell should be the persistent attacker of Churchill from the Opposition Front Bench.

This position was inevitable. During the war Shinwell, although refusing to join Bevan's attacks, was one of the lonely critics of the Government. In the Socialist Government he was Minister of Fuel and Power (during the period of the coal crisis of 1947), Minister of War and finally Minister of Defence. This latter post brought him into the field of defence policy for which he was often roundly criticized by Churchill. When Churchill assumed the mantle of Minister of Defence upon becoming Prime Minister the roles were reversed. Since there is a continuity in defence policy whichever party is in power, Shinwell could therefore find himself in a strong position to score points.

Shinwell did not fail to do battle, opening with an exchange upon the North Atlantic Treaty Organization in which he asked a question regarding its strength.

THE PRIME MINISTER: *The disclosure of information as regards the forces at the disposal of the North Atlantic Council is a matter for that body. At its recent meeting in Paris the Council decided to confine itself to what is said in the second paragraph of the communiqué issued on 20th April. It would clearly be inappropriate for a member Government to make available more detailed information than that agreed upon by the Council.*

MR SHINWELL [Labour]: *As we find it very difficult to obtain any detailed information about what is going on, is it not the duty of the right hon. Gentleman not to try to evade Questions put to him, as he did the previous Question, but to face up to them and give us some information? How are we to get the information otherwise? We ask a Question and there are evasive answers or reticence on the part of the right hon. Gentleman. What are we to do? Are we to go to Paris and ask the questions?*

THE PRIME MINISTER: *The right hon. Gentleman was one of the architects of NATO and if he chooses to go to*

*Paris and address that body or any representatives with whom
he could come in contact no objection would be taken.*

MR SHINWELL: *Perhaps the right hon. Gentleman will
accompany me when I go. May I ask him whether he recalls
that when he sat on this side of the House and we sat on the
Government side he was constantly asking for information of
a detailed character, and when we occasionally said that in the
interests of security it was not desirable to give it he said,
'Why do you always claim that it is in the public interest not
to divulge information?' What is the position now? Has he
changed his outlook on these matters?*

THE PRIME MINISTER: *It seems to be uncommonly like the
position of the right hon. Gentleman.*

[*Hansard*, 18 *May* 1953, *col.* 1706]

This was a continuation of earlier contests when Sir
Winston Churchill might have been thought to have been
on very unsafe ground indeed. During the term of the
Socialist Government he bitterly reproached it for agreeing
to an American Supreme Commander for the Atlantic. At
the same time he stated that he was in favour of an American
overall commander for the Mediterranean. Naturally his
political opponents seized the opportunity.

MR R. T. PAGET [Labour] *asked the Prime Minister if
he has any statement to make on the Mediterranean naval
command.*

THE PRIME MINISTER: *I am not at present in a position to
make any statement on this subject.*

MR PAGET: *Will the Prime Minister agree that continued
American interest in the Mediterranean is vital to us here and
it is also vital to our security that the Mediterranean should
have an adequate allocation of Atlantic Mediterranean force?*

Has the right hon. Gentleman seen in the 'Daily Express' today, under the banner headline 'U.S. Admiral rejected. Britain: We must rule Med.', the statement: 'Admiral William Fechteler . . . will be told at a Defence Ministry round-table conference in Whitehall today that the British Government cannot agree to the appointment of U.S. Admiral Robert B. Carney as Mediterranean Supreme Commander? Is that statement true and, if it is true, is that likely to maintain American interests in the Mediterranean?

THE PRIME MINISTER: *I think the House will agree that that somewhat lengthy supplementary is fully covered by my original answer.*

MR CALLAGHAN [Labour]: *Will the right hon. Gentleman agree to give the House an assurance that his view remains unchanged from 19th April last year when he told us that on high military and national grounds he would prefer an American commander in the Mediterranean?*

THE PRIME MINISTER: *My views –* [HON. MEMBERS: *Have changed.*] *A harmonious process which keeps them in relation to the current movement of events.*

MR SHINWELL [Labour]: *Will the right hon. Gentleman mind addressing himself to the question a little more seriously? Does he not appreciate that this is a very serious matter affecting the naval command of the Mediterranean and determining the status of the British Navy? Does he not recall the occasion of* 19th *April last year when I, on behalf of the Labour Government –*

THE PRIME MINISTER: *Gave way on the command of the Atlantic.*

MR SHINWELL: *Does he not recall that I stated that our intention was to see that we remained in naval control of the Mediterranean and the right hon. Gentleman rejected that view and asserted that it was a proper location for the United States Command? Could he say what is the position of Her Majesty's Government now?*

THE PRIME MINISTER: *I thought I had already just said I was not in a position to make a statement on that matter today.*

MR SHINWELL: *Are we to understand that the right hon. Gentleman is going to sell the pass? Do I understand that, not only has he changed his mind, but he is going to hand over naval control of the Mediterranean to the United States Government? Is this to be a complete monopoly for the United States?*

THE PRIME MINISTER: *I really do not think I have anything to add to what I have said. I am sure the House would not wish me to be provoked by the taunts of an uneasy conscience.*   [*Hansard,* 5 *May* 1952, *col.* 32]

This was an almost perfect example of Churchill's overwhelming Parliamentary manner. He was equally masterly when, nine days later, the matter was raised again with a repetition of many of the phrases – to demonstrate how they had stung. The Prime Minister was asked by Mr Shinwell whether he could state the divergence of view between the United States Government and Her Majesty's Government on the Naval command in the Mediterranean. After some exchanges Mr Shinwell asked if there were any reason why the House should not be informed what H.M. Government thought about the naval command in the Mediterranean.

THE PRIME MINISTER: *Yes. The reason is that the discussions are now proceeding on a staff level, which may end the whole matter. If not, the Governments will be drawn in, and other decisions will have to be taken.*

MR SHINWELL [Labour]: *Is not this an indication of the right hon. Gentleman's uneasy conscience in this matter?*

THE PRIME MINISTER: *On the contrary, my conscience is absolutely easy. I do not feel in any danger of selling the pass, considering that the largest pass was sold by the right hon. Gentleman.*

MR SHINWELL: *Does the right hon. Gentleman recall that he stated quite categorically in this House in the course of debate, or at any rate in the course of Question and answer, that he thought the Americans had the right to assume the naval command in the Mediterranean, in spite of this being a traditionally British area?*

THE PRIME MINISTER: *That is a very inadequate representation of the views which I expressed at great length and which I have here fully on this subject.*

MR SHINWELL: *Read them.*

THE PRIME MINISTER: *No, thank you very much. I should be delighted to refer the right hon. Gentleman to Hansard: I wonder his curiosity has not already led him to investigate. The situation now is different from what it was a year ago. Very important decisions were taken by the right hon. Gentleman and his colleagues which we must take into consideration in dealing with future circumstances.*

MR JAMES CALLAGHAN [Labour]: *Does not the Prime Minister think it is really sinking below the level of events to talk about the military arrangements in terms of selling the pass? May I ask him whether he does not think it is highly undesirable that these Admirals should go about making statements on matters which concern staff conversations? Would it*

*not be far better to reserve the statements to be made by Gov-
ernments in due course?*

THE PRIME MINISTER: *I do not know whether the hon.
Gentleman realizes that he is passing a very strict, direct,
pointed and severe censure upon the former Minister of Defence, who quite gratuitously the other day, on these grave
matters, introduced such a disgusting expression as 'selling the
pass' and tried, with conspicuous ill success, to fasten it on to
me.* [Hansard, 14 May 1952, col. 1438]

On the subject of General Eisenhower's resignation as
Supreme Commander in Europe, Mr Shinwell, after pressing
that his successor should not necessarily be an American,
asked that the House might be entitled to express its
opinion before Mr Churchill made up his mind.

THE PRIME MINISTER: *If I remember rightly, the decision
on the American Admiral* [made by Shinwell] *was announced without the House being told about it beforehand.
The right hon. Gentleman must be very careful not, by a
refinement of unreason, to manage to be wrong both times.*
[Hansard, 1 April 1952, col. 1412]

Shinwell possesses many of the outward signs of the dema-
gogue, although tempered by a humorous sense of propor-
tion which prevents any temptation to real excess. Although
he is naturally shy, he can be induced into a Parliamentary
style even when moved in private conversation. He has a
ready public wit and his tongue can be acid. In 1935 he
defeated Ramsay MacDonald at Seaham in an election which,
tradition holds, rose to heights of vituperation. Shinwell
claims that he did not attack MacDonald personally but there
can be no comparison between scoring points off a softened,
failing MacDonald and off Winston Churchill at the height

of his Parliamentary brilliance. It can only be said that if Shinwell has anything to show in the way of success in his exchanges it is when he has succeeded in goading the Prime Minister into losing his temper.

Winston Churchill's temper is, to put it mildly, not one to be relied upon. He has got past the age – if he ever arrived at it – when he could suffer fools gladly. At Strasbourg in 1950, he stigmatized some of his own supporters, whom he regarded as too timid in action, as 'lily-livered hares'. Upon occasion, the wasp-like persistency of Shinwell has caused Churchill to lose his temper. One was when the Prime Minister defended Lord Alexander for remarks made in a speech at the Canada Club, which contained 'confidential references' not made in the House of Lords. It was a hot afternoon and the Opposition took full advantage of a good tactical situation.

MR SHINWELL [Labour]: *May I ask the right hon. Gentleman whether Lord Alexander, who did, apparently, quite honestly and conscientiously regard this matter as secret and confidential – as, indeed, he said – conveyed this information to the Prime Minister; and what did the Prime Minister instruct him to do?*

THE PRIME MINISTER: *I was not consulted.* [HON. MEMBERS: *Oh.*] *Why should I be? I have never been consulted on details of every statement which is made –*

MR SHINWELL: *This was a secret statement.*

THE PRIME MINISTER: *– but if he had asked me, I should have said, 'Make it in the House of Lords. It can do no possible harm. It is true and thoroughly guarded by your other remarks.' That is what I should have said.*

MR SHINWELL: *I repeat the question, and perhaps the right hon. Gentleman would be good enough to give a straight answer.*

THE PRIME MINISTER: *I am dealing with the right hon. Gentleman on a perfectly fair and square level and giving full and clear answers. That he should suggest that I vary my answers between what is straight and what is not straight is worthy of his own mind and worthy only of his own mind.*

MR SHINWELL: *Does the right hon. Gentleman realize that we recognize that the reason he is losing his temper is that he is in a position of great difficulty from which he cannot extricate himself? Is he aware that he has accused hon. and right hon. Members on this side of lack of tact and that now, when he is asked about one of his Ministers 'dropping a brick', he loses his temper? Whether the right hon. Gentleman regards it as impudent or not, he has got to give a straight and truthful answer to the House.*

THE PRIME MINISTER *rose –*

MR SHINWELL: *Wait a minute.*

HON. MEMBERS: *Withdraw.*

MR SPEAKER: *I think the heat outside is affecting this discussion, and I will ask hon. and right hon. Gentlemen to keep any unnecessary heat out of their questions.*

[*Hansard*, 2 July 1952, *col.* 434]

Several months later a series of exchanges on the Mediterranean Supreme Commander led Churchill into a heavy – and perhaps unseemly – riposte which drew upon him the full fire of the Opposition.

MR SHINWELL [Labour]: *Does the Prime Minister seriously suggest to the House that after six months –* [AN HON. MEMBER: *Seven.*] *– or seven months – what is a matter of a month to the right hon. Gentleman? – after a long period of time he is unable to come to a conclusion upon a matter upon which he expressed quite definite opinions when he was on* *this side of the House? Why can he not make up his mind?*

THE PRIME MINISTER: *I long ago made up my mind: the question is to get other people to agree. I hope to make a statement on this matter when we meet after Christmas and after the conferences now taking place in Paris, and I would, if I might be permitted by the indulgence of the House, warn the right hon. Gentleman not to be too prophetic about the way in which things are going. They may not all be as unfortunate for this country as he would no doubt wish.*

HON. MEMBERS: *Withdraw.*

[*Hansard, 3 Dec. 1952, col. 1569*]

Attempts were made by Mr Mitchison and Mr Attlee to get the Prime Minister to withdraw this remark. He, however, while amending the sting of his remark, would not do so. The result was felt quite soon afterwards when the House considered the Transport Bill in Committee and members of the Socialist Party booed the Prime Minister.

HON. MEMBERS: *Boo.*

THE CHAIRMAN: *I hope that the Committee will behave more quietly.*

THE PRIME MINISTER: *On a point of order. Is it in order to boo a Member of this House?*

MR WILLIAM ROSS [Labour]: *What else can you say to a goose?*

THE CHAIRMAN: *The hon. Member must withdraw that remark.*

Much discussion followed as to whether the word 'goose' were a Parliamentary expression or not. Mr Churchill finally said that he did not in the least mind being called a goose. He had been called many worse things than that. Despite a further intervention by Mr Aneurin Bevan the matter rested there. Shinwell took no part in any of the protest which the Prime Minister's words called forth.

In a discussion on the Suez Canal area:

THE PRIME MINISTER: *I should, of course, treat with great attention anything he might say upon the subject of contradictory statements by politicians or Ministers. He is a past master of the art himself.* [*Hansard, 28 Oct. 1952, col. 1747*]

'Does the Prime Minister seriously suggest . . . ?'

A Question by Mr Shinwell on ammunition was prompted by a statement made by a retiring General (General Van Fleet) in Korea.

THE PRIME MINISTER: *I have to rely upon the official information which is transmitted to us in due course. I cannot deal with every statement that is made by an ex-commander – or even by an ex-Cabinet Minister.*
[*Hansard, 26 March 1953, col. 834*]

Mr Shinwell, in the course of questions as to who would answer questions on atomic energy in the House of Commons, indicated that 'some of us' would be glad to relieve Mr Churchill of all political responsibility.

THE PRIME MINISTER: *I think that is rather ungrateful. I must have been too complimentary to the right hon. Gentleman. He has explained what harm any compliment from me did to him. I must really rake up a few more compliments.*
[*Hansard, 17 Nov. 1953, col. 1573*]

When Mr Shinwell inquired whether he could put down questions on the National Service Act from month to month:

THE PRIME MINISTER: *I should never attempt to inflict upon the right hon. Gentleman such limitations upon his curiosity.*   [*Hansard, 24 Nov. 1953, col. 195*]

The Socialist Mr Dodds had asked a question about the arrangement of a meeting with Mr Malenkov which Mr Churchill had already answered on the previous Monday in reply to the Acting Leader of the Opposition, Mr Herbert Morrison.

THE PRIME MINISTER: *I am afraid – I do not want to be unfair – but I am afraid I must leave this to be settled between the hon. Member, who is seeking political advancement, and the Acting Leader of the Opposition.*
MR SHINWELL [Labour] *rose –*
THE PRIME MINISTER: *You are the Leader now, are you?*

Mr Shinwell's reply should be given if only as a yardstick of the two minds and vocabularies.

MR SHINWELL: *I see no reason why the right hon. Gentleman should be so nasty. I merely want to ask a question which*

may interest him. Perhaps he had better wait for the question
before he indulges in these rude interjections . . .
                              [*Hansard, 22 April 1953, col.* 1171]

Mr Shinwell enjoys the dubious political advantage of
being known to his intimates and a wide outer fringe of
Socialist supporters as 'Manny'. He has in his time been
much hated by his political opponents (was he not merchant
of those phrases 'two hoots' and 'tinker's cuss' as a member
of the Government after the war?), but in these days, at the
age of seventy, he has almost achieved a cosy respectability.
It is recalled that he has always stuck to his principles and
that, although quick-tempered, he is really a nice man at
heart. There is even some evidence that Churchill, in his
mellow moments, recognizes Mr Shinwell's qualities.

In a debate upon United States Air Force Bases in the
United Kingdom :

MR SHINWELL [Labour] : *In case there should be any mis-*
understanding about the official policy of the Parliamentary
Labour Party, may I ask the right hon. Gentleman whether
he is aware that the decision taken by the late Government in
the light of the then international circumstances, which are
apparently still prevailing so far as we know, was a decision
from which at present we are not prepared to run away?

THE PRIME MINISTER: *I think that these statements made*
by responsible ex-Ministers on the Front Opposition Bench
are a valuable contribution to our debate.
                              [*Hansard, 9 Feb.* 1954*, col.* 1001]

What, in fact, do Sir Winston Churchill and Mr Emanuel
Shinwell think of each other? The House of Commons is a
small world of its own in which, with its crowded conditions, the architect Barry has now left very little room for

private animosity. The Prime Minister and Mr Shinwell do not in the course of events meet a great deal outside the Floor of the House. The story is told, however, of the two of them being seen together. Mr Shinwell was gesticulating strenuously and it seemed that at last their personal exchanges had reached a violent stage. Approached closer, Mr Shinwell's words could be heard. He was saying, 'But why didn't you *tell* me your horse was going to win?'

To conclude on what is probably the right note:

MR SHINWELL [Labour]: *May I enquire whether the right hon. Gentleman is in a better temper than I understand he was early this morning?*

THE PRIME MINISTER: *Because I show robust energy, it does not follow that I have a sensitive or injured disposition.*

[*Hansard, 23 April 1953, col. 1403*]

His Victims' Verdict

Winston Churchill has lacerated many an ego in the House of Commons. Yet when he became a Knight of the Garter in 1953, there was consternation even among those who had frequently been his targets. For usually only members of the House of Lords, 'the other place' in the Palace of Westminster, are made Knights of the Garter. Was this a sign that the Commons were about to lose him?

MR EMRYS HUGHES [Labour]: *May I ask the Prime Minister, more in sorrow than in anger, whether he will give an assurance that he is not on the slippery slope to another place?*

THE PRIME MINISTER: *Provided the term 'another place' is used in the strictly Parliamentary sense, I will gladly give the assurance required.* [Hansard, 24 April 1953, col. 1764]

A Member who has often felt the sting of his wit also added an appreciation. The occasion was Sir Winston's first appearance in the House after his severe illness in 1953.

MR WOODROW WYATT [Labour]: *May I ask the Prime Minister whether he is aware that the House of Commons is a duller place without him?*
[*Hansard,* 20 Oct. 1953, *col.* 1807]

To this Sir Winston Churchill, nearly a year later, added a further word. There had been much talk in the newspapers of his retirement: much pressure had been expended in an effort to make him resign. In the summer of 1954, however, he had a drink at the House of Commons with an old journalist friend.

'What are they saying about me these days?' asked Churchill.

'Well, quite frankly, quite a few of your Conservative friends are saying that it would be a good thing for the party if you were to resign some time fairly soon.'

Churchill glanced about him.

'You know, as I look at this room and think back over my long association with this House, I think this is a pretty good pub.'

And he added: 'And as I look at the faces in the House, I wonder why I should leave this pub until someone says, "Time, please!" – in somewhat stronger accents than those of my friends to whom you have been speaking.'